GRILLMASTER

GRILLMASTER

The ultimate tips, techniques, and recipes for the perfect barbecue

METRO BOOKS
New York

An Imprint of Sterling Publishing
387 Park Avenue South
New York, NY 10016

Written by: Lovoni Walker with thanks to Lawrence Imrie
Project Editors: Catherine Knight and Helen Caldon
Art Director: Susi Martin
Publisher: James Tavendale

All photography by Bruce Nimmer with the exception of the following: front and back cover, p2, p9, p10 p13, p14, p20, p21, p22, p27, p28, p30, p42, p52, p76, p78, p103, p120, 122, p138, p154, p156, p174, p182, p186, p188, p210, p232, p234, p236, p241 Shutterstock.com

ISBN 978-1-4351-4542-9

For information about custom editions, special sales, and premium and corporate purchases, please contact Sterling Special Sales at 800-805-5489 or specialsales@sterlingpublishing.com.

Manufactured in China

2 4 6 8 10 9 7 5 3 1

www.sterlingpublishing.com

CONTENTS

INTRODUCTION

Cooking food over open coals is a tradition that goes back centuries. Originally practiced by our ancestors out of necessity, now we gather around a glowing grill with friends and family to relax, enjoy each other's company, and eat delicious food.

Barbecuing has evolved into a cooking style all of its own. Around the world, different grilling techniques have developed, take for example the American "pit" where low and slow is the name of the game, then there's the South African "braii," or the great Aussie "barbie" for sizzle in the sunshine. Although all vary, the basics are the same and have remained so for thousands of years.

The recipes in this book will show you the best of what the world of outdoor cooking has to offer. Full of tasty suggestions for meats, vegetables, sides, and marinades, you'll find tried and tested favorites from around the globe as well as new and exciting ideas. Perfect for both beginners and those looking to develop their grilling skills, these recipes are not limited to summertime and sunshine and you'll soon find that you're cooking outdoors all year round.

Sales of barbecues really began to take off in the second half of the twentieth century and the variety of barbecues that you have to choose from these days has increased dramatically.

A charcoal barbecue has to be the purist's choice as it's the closest thing to cooking in the wild. Charcoal cooking is a great way to get back to nature and reconnect with your inner caveman, provided you don't mind a little mess and have the patience to wait until the coals are ready before you start cooking.

Look for a grill that has a lid and vents top and bottom, as this makes for better temperature control and gives you the opportunity to try hot smoking (indirect cooking) as your barbecuing skills develop. A built-in temperature gauge is also handy.

Of course the flavor of food from a charcoal barbecue is better too, isn't it?Well, actually that's open to debate. That distinctive smoky barbecue flavor has nothing to do with the smoke from the charcoal. In fact it comes from the smoke created when juices and fat in the food drip onto the hot coals and vaporize. Modern gas barbecues mimic this process beautifully with flavor bars that sit between the gas burner and the cooking grate. In blind taste tests, many top barbecue chefs have preferred food cooked on a gas barbecue to that cooked on charcoal.

So pick the barbecue that's right for you, collect a few basic tools, choose from this brilliant selection of recipes and gather your friends, you're ready to get grilling. Fire up the barbie!

BARBECUING ESSENTIALS

Follow these simple steps and burnt sausages, undercooked chicken, and eyebrow-singeing flareups will soon be things of the past.

The Basics

It's always tempting to be "doing something" when barbecue grilling, but sometimes it's best to stand back and let the barbecue do the work.

• Every time you flip a piece of meat you cool the side that was starting to cook. Fight the temptation to flip and try to turn it just once.
• Resist the urge to squeeze your spatula and press down on food such as burgers and steaks. All this does is drive out the moisture and make the end result dry.
• Don't prick food – this is just another way to dry it out. Meat should cook in its fat, that's what adds the flavor.
• Season steaks on one side only. When searing a steak you want a really hot grill and the seasoning acts as a heat barrier.
• Use a marinade as it will add flavor and succulence to your cooking. A little sugar in the marinade tenderizes meat.

Lighting a Charcoal Grill

Charcoal grills are easy to light if you know the tricks of the trade. Depending on the type of grill you have bought there will be a top grate (for cooking food) and either a lower grate for charcoal or maybe just the base of the barbecue unit. This area is known as the firebox. Remove the upper cooking grate before you place your charcoal in position. Generally speaking, barbecues that have a lower charcoal grate are best fuelled with charcoal briquettes. There are three main ways to light charcoal:

1. A chimney starter is a metal cylinder with a charcoal grate mounted inside. Unlit charcoal is placed in the top of the cylinder and newspaper at the bottom, under the grate. When the newspaper is lit, it burns and lights the charcoal above. The "chimney effect" causes the charcoal to light from the bottom all the way up to the top. It will take 10–20 minutes for the coals to light, depending on wind conditions, how much charcoal is in the chimney, and the type of charcoal being used. The charcoal is ready when you see an orange color deep inside the chimney starter, flames licking at the charcoal at the top of the chimney, and gray ash just starting to form on some of the charcoal at the top. At this point you can pour it into the base of your barbecue.

2. An alternative method is to use a poker lighter. These either take the shape of a propane torch or they can be electrically powered (like a big soldering iron). Light the torch and insert the starter into the coals for the amount of time recommended by the manufacturer. When done, remove the starter and place it on a heatproof surface until cool.

3. The final option is to use fire-lighter cubes, gel, or lighter fluid. When using gel or lighter fluid apply it to the charcoal according to the manufacturer's instructions and once lit do not be tempted to add any more once the fire has started. Make sure that any residue has fully burned off before placing any food on the grate to minimize the petrochemical taste. Instant lighting charcoal has its uses if you are traveling because the charcoal comes in easy to handle packs, but that's about the only redeeming feature.

Once the charcoal is lit, the coals need time to settle, so a little patience is required. The coals are ready to cook on when the flames have died down and the coals are gray in color. If meat is placed on the cooking grate before the coals are ready then there will be a high risk of a flare up and a subsequent burnt offering.

Lighting a Gas Grill

The golden rule when lighting a gas grill for the first time is to read the manufacturer's instructions. After that there are several safety rules to follow every time you light up:

- Check that there is enough fuel in your gas tank.
- Ensure that all burner control knobs are off.
- Turn the gas on at the source and light the burners.
- Once lit, close the lid to let the flavor bars get up to temperature. This usually takes about 10 minutes.
- Use a long-armed wire brush to dust down your cooking grate. This is easier to do when the grill is still hot.

Testing the Grill Temperature

Most barbecues that have a lid attached will also have an in-built thermometer gauge. Don't worry if yours doesn't, they're not expensive to buy and are a good investment if you plan to do a lot of barbecuing. If you haven't got a grill thermometer there's an easy way to estimate the temperature. Hold your hand palm-side down over the area where you are going to cook your food and count the seconds. Be very careful to not hold your hand too near the heat source, the aim is not to burn yourself!

Time	Approx Temperature
1 second	Very Hot
2 seconds	Hot
3 seconds	Medium-Hot
4 seconds	Medium
5 seconds	Medium-Low
6 seconds	Low

Cooking Methods

Direct

This is where food is placed on the cooking grate directly over a solid area of heat, such as a bed of hot coals or a gas burner. In this environment the food needs to be turned so that all sides cook evenly.

Indirect

Here the heat source is restricted to the edges of the firebox, leaving a space clear in the center for a drip tray or water bath, the food is then placed on the cooking grate over the drip tray. Indirect cooking is only possible on a lidded barbecue. With charcoal barbecues the coals are placed on the opposite sides of the firebox whereas with gas barbecues the food is placed in the center of the cooking grate and the peripheral burners used to provide heat.

The lid of the barbecue acts as a heat reflector so the food doesn't need to be turned as often during cooking. This method is ideal for cooking large pieces of meat like whole chickens, racks of ribs, or pork shoulder.

Try to not lift the lid too often because the heat will escape and you'll add to the cooking every time you take a peek.

Spit Roasting

Some barbecue grills come with a spit-roasting attachment. The meat is skewered onto the spit rod and secured by two adjustable forks that slide up and down the rod, one on either side. The meat is placed over the heat (some gas barbecues have the heat source vertically mounted at the back of the grill) and the spit rod rotates, cooking the meat evenly on all sides.

Using Wood Chips to Add Flavor

In addition to the smoke from the meat juices you can further enhance the barbecue flavor by adding more wood smoke of your own. Hardwood chips are now available in most stores where barbecues are sold and some of the popular varieties include hickory, mesquite, oak, apple, or cherry. All citrus woods are good, as are most hard woods; the ones to avoid are softwoods and birch. In order to get the most out of wood chips, soak them for 30 minutes before cooking begins. They can then be sprinkled directly onto the charcoal fire.

For gas barbecues, take the soaked wood chips and wrap them in aluminum foil. Make some puncture holes in the foil then rest the pack on the flavor bars. Other options for adding flavor include:

- Dry twigs from fruit trees or vine cuttings.
- Woody stalks from herbs such as rosemary, thyme, or bay.
- Leftover almond, walnut, or hazelnut shells that have been soaked for 30 minutes.
- Seaweed (when cooking fish or seafood).

Buying The Right Tools

It's worth stating the obvious here: barbecues are hot and so having tools with long handles is essential. This list of tools is not exhaustive but includes all the basic equipment you need.

Wide metal spatula – used for turning chicken pieces, vegetables, and smaller pieces of food.

Long-handled grill brush – used for cleaning the grill grates whilst the grill is hot.

Use brass bristles on a porcelain enamel grate and steel bristles on a cast-iron grate.

Basting brush – used for basting food. Get one with natural bristles as nylon will melt if it gets too hot.

Tongs – used for turning sausages, shellfish, kebabs, etc. Don't buy the tongs with serrated teeth because every time you turn food you'll prick it, release the juices and dry it out.

Fork – used for lifting cooked food off the grate.

Gloves – heat resistant to protect your hands. For extra protection to your forearms, consider a gauntlet.

Skewers – Great for holding small pieces of meat and kebabs. If using bamboo skewers, they need to be soaked for 30 minutes prior to threading and cooking. Metal skewers need to be long and reasonably thick to make turning meat easier.

Meat Thermometer – perfect for ensuring that your meat is cooked. Look for an instant-read digital probe.

Barbecue Baskets – hinged wire baskets ideal for cooking fish. The baskets quickly turn it over without the fish sticking or breaking up.

Avoiding Flareups

Fat on meat is necessary for adding flavor but occasionally fat will drip and cause a flareup. These should be avoided as much as possible as they can wreck a great meal in seconds. Remember, it is heat that cooks food, flames only burn it. To avoid flareups:

- Trim excess fat from meat (but leave at least ¼ in/5 mm) before it is placed on the grill.
- If the grill has a height setting for cooking, always start on the highest rung.
- Only light the charcoal under 75% of the cooking grate, this leaves 25% of the grate free as a cool zone where you can place food out of the way of the flames.
- Have a water spray handy so that you can douse the flames. If using a charcoal grill, try filling the water spray with apple juice. Not only will it control the flare ups but it will also add a sweet coating to your food that will caramelize in the heat.

Testing for "Doneness"

Using a meat thermometer will guarantee that your meat is done to perfection every time.

The instant-read variety allows you to check a number of places in the meat in quick succession. When reading a thermometer the sensor probe should not touch any fat, bone, or the grill and generally speaking it should be inserted into the thickest area of the meat.

If a thermometer is not available then you can use sight and touch.

- For red meat, cut into the meat and check the color inside.
- For poultry, prick the meat with a skewer and see what color the juices run. If they are clear, the meat is done.

Using the touch method

Using touch is really helpful with red meats, especially steaks. Using your right thumb and index finger, feel the chunk of flesh at the base of your left thumb.

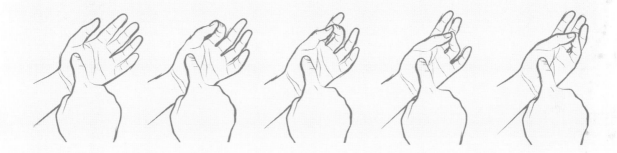

Rare

The center is bright red, raw, and is at room temperature. The texture will be the same as that piece of flesh at the base of your thumb if your left hand is relaxed.

Medium-rare

The center is red but doesn't look raw. Bring the tips of your left thumb and index finger together in an "OK" sign. A medium-rare steak will feel the same as the flesh at the base of your left thumb when the thumb and index finger are touching.

Medium

The center of the meat is pink and the feel of the meat is like the base of your thumb when your thumb and middle finger tip are touching.

Medium-well

The middle of the meat will be ever so slightly pink and the springiness similar to the base of your thumb when your thumb and ring finger are touching.

Well done

No pink color in the center of the meat and it will be firm to the touch, like the base of your thumb when your little finger and thumb are touching.

Barbecue Safety

Here are some quick pointers to ensure that you have a happy and safe cooking experience:

- Read the manufacturer's instructions carefully before assembling your new barbecue.
- If using gas, ensure that you have the correct regulator and fuel supply.
- Make sure your barbecue is on level ground, is sturdy and doesn't wobble.
- Keep your barbecue 10 feet away from any combustible materials, including the house, garage, and fences.
- Never use the BBQ indoors or under a covered patio or car port.
- Never try to start a barbecue in high winds.
- Keep children and pets out of the way.
- Do not add lighter fluid to a lit fire.
- Never add charcoal to a gas barbecue.
- Use heat-resistant gloves and long-handled tools.
- Do not spray oil onto a hot cooking grate, spray it on the food instead.
- Don't line the bottom of your barbecue with aluminum foil, this will obstruct airflow and act as a grease trap which can then flare up.
- When finished, close the lid on the barbecue, close the vents and if gas, turn off the gas supply.
- Never extinguish a charcoal barbecue by throwing cold water on it. This will cause the firebox to contract rapidly and it may crack. Porcelain enamelled surfaces may shatter.
- Do not store propane tanks indoors or in the garage

Cleaning Your Barbecue

It pays to keep your cooking grate clean. After each cook-out (and when it has cooled), scrape the cooking grate with a wire brush. Use a brush with brass bristles on a porcelain enamel grill and steel bristles on a cast-iron grate.

When you've got the majority of the residue off, give the grates a soak in warm soapy water and then finish off with an abrasive soap-filled scouring pad. Remove any ash from the charcoal firebox on a regular basis. Ash collects moisture and will cause it to rust if left.

Additionally for gas barbecues:

Keep your gas barbecue away from moisture and protect it from rust. Rust inside the burners can cause blockages or dust particles in the flames. In both cases this will result in incomplete combustion of the propane and may result in sooty deposits on your food. A tell-tale sign that you have a problem is if the flame on your burner is more orange than the normal blue.

The cooking grates, drip trays, and burners all need the warm soapy water treatment. A grill cover is a great accessory to protect your barbecue from the elements if you are planning to keep it outside all year round.

BEEF & LAMB

A barbecue wouldn't be complete without a selection of succulent red meat. In this chapter, you'll find there's so much more to barbecued beef than a few burgers, and you didn't need to limit lamb to a kebab. Who could turn down a juicy Grilled Steak with Horseradish Butter, or divine Honey-Glazed Lamb? Try these recipes and you'll have your guests lining up for second helpings of Feta Lamb Burgers, Beef Satay, Chilli-Crusted Beef and many more meaty treats—whether you pass on the recipes is up to you!

STEAK WITH HORSERADISH BUTTER AND ROSEMARY FRIES

PREHEAT THE OVEN TO 425°F/220°C/gas mark 7.

To make the butter, combine the butter, horseradish, and garlic in a bowl and season with salt and pepper. Spoon the mixture onto a sheet of greaseproof paper and roll into a log, using the paper to help you. Refrigerate until firm.

Place the chips and rosemary on a baking sheet, season well and toss to combine. Bake according to the packet instructions.

Heat the barbecue to medium-high (about 400°F/200°C/gas mark 6). Brush the steaks with oil and season with salt and pepper. Grill the steaks on the barbecue for about 3 minutes on each side or until cooked to your liking.

Slice the chilled horseradish butter and place a couple of slices on each steak. Serve with the rosemary fries.

SERVES 4

½ stick (60g) butter, softened
2 tablespoons creamed
  horseradish
1 garlic clove, crushed
salt and freshly ground black
  pepper
1 lb 5 oz (600 g) frozen French
fries
3 rosemary sprigs
4 x 10 oz (300 g) rib eye steaks
olive oil, for brushing

FETA LAMB BURGERS

1 lb 2 oz (500 g) lamb mince
2 garlic cloves, crushed
salt and freshly ground black
  pepper
olive oil, for brushing
4 burger buns, split
½ cup (115 ml) natural yogurt
a handful of fresh mint leaves,
  finely chopped
1 red onion, finely chopped
6 oz (175 g) feta cheese
2 tomatoes, sliced
a handful of baby spinach leaves

HEAT THE BARBECUE TO MEDIUM (about 350°F/180°C/gas mark 4) and grease the grill.

Combine the mince, garlic, salt and pepper in a bowl and mix well to combine. Divide the mixture into four and shape into patties. Brush each patty with oil and grill for 3–4 minutes on each side until cooked through. Remove from the grill, set aside and keep warm.

Toast the buns on the barbecue for 1 minute or until golden.

Combine the yogurt, mint, and onion in bowl then spread the mixture on the toasted buns. Top with the burgers, feta, tomatoes, and spinach leaves to serve.

SERVES 4

HERB-CRUSTED VEAL

HEAT THE BARBECUE TO MEDIUM-HIGH (about 400°F/200°C/gas mark 6) and grease the grill.

Season the veal with salt and pepper then set aside.

Combine the remaining ingredients in a bowl then spread over the veal using your fingers or a spoon.

Grill the veal on the barbecue for 20 minutes with the barbecue lid closed for medium-rare meat, a few minutes longer for well done.

Cover the veal with aluminum foil and allow to rest for 10 minutes before slicing.

SERVES 6

2 lb 4 oz (1 kg) veal loin
salt and freshly ground black
  pepper
3 tablespoons chopped flat leaf
  parsley
3 tablespoons chopped chives
2 tablespoons Dijon mustard
1 tablespoon lemon juice

LAMB, EGGPLANT, AND FETA SALAD

To make the sesame orange dressing, combine all the ingredients in a screw-top jar and shake well.

Heat the barbecue to medium-high (400°F/200°C/gas mark 6).

Drizzle the lamb shanks with olive oil and season with salt and pepper. Cook on the barbecue, using indirect heat and with the lid closed, for 1–1½ hours until tender. Set aside until cool enough to handle then remove the meat from bones and coarsely chop.

Brush the eggplant slices with oil. Grill on the barbecue for about 4 minutes on each side until the flesh has softened and grill marks appear. Remove from the grill and cut into large pieces.

Gently mix together the lamb, eggplant, feta, mint, and cilantro in a bowl. Drizzle with the dressing and toss to combine. Sprinkle with toasted almonds before serving.

Serves 4

SESAME ORANGE DRESSING
3 tablespoons olive oil
2 garlic cloves, crushed
¼ teaspoon sesame oil
2 tablespoons orange juice
2 tablespoons white wine
   vinegar
¼ teaspoon ground cumin
salt and freshly ground black
   pepper

3 lamb shanks
olive oil
salt and freshly ground black
   pepper
2 eggplants, sliced horizontally
3 oz (90 g) feta cheese, crumbled
3 tablespoons chopped mint
a handful of fresh cilantro
3 oz (85 g) silvered almonds,
   toasted

CHEESE AND TOMATO VEAL STEAKS

4 thin veal steaks
1 teaspoon vegetable oil
salt and freshly ground black
  pepper
2 oz (55 g) olive tapenade
4 slices Swiss cheese
2 medium vine-ripened tomatoes,
  sliced
8 basil leaves
baby arugula leaves, to serve
balsamic vinegar, to serve

HEAT THE BARBECUE TO MEDIUM-HIGH (about 400°F/200°C/gas mark 6) and grease the grill. Soak 12 cocktail sticks in a bowl of water.

Place the veal steaks between layers of plastic wrap. Using a rolling pin, gently pound the meat to about ¼ in/6 mm thick. Brush the veal with oil and season with salt and pepper.

Spread one side of each piece of veal with tapenade then add the cheese, sliced tomato, and basil to one half. Fold the veal over to cover the filling. Secure with the cocktail sticks.

Grill the veal on the barbecue for 3–4 minutes on each side until cooked through. Remove the cocktail sticks before serving. Serve with arugula leaves drizzled with balsamic vinegar.

SERVES 4

MINTED LAMB LEG

COMBINE THE OIL, VINEGAR, SUGAR, mint, salt and pepper in shallow dish. Add the lamb and turn to coat in the mixture. Cover and refrigerate for 1 hour.

Heat the barbecue to medium-high (about 400°F/200°C/gas mark 6) then reduce the heat to low (about 275°F/140°C/gas mark 1). Grease the grill.

Place the lamb on the barbecue and close the lid. For medium-rare meat, cook for 40 minutes, turning halfway through. Thicker meat will require slightly longer. Remove the lamb from the grill, cover with aluminum foil and allow to rest for 10 minutes before slicing.

TO MAKE THE MINT SAUCE, combine all the ingredients in a bowl. Serve with the lamb.

SERVES 6

¼ cup (55 ml) olive oil
¼ cup (55 ml) malt vinegar
1 tablespoon soft brown sugar
a handful of fresh mint leaves, chopped
salt and freshly ground black pepper
2 lb 4 oz (1 kg) butterflied leg of lamb

MINT SAUCE
¼ cup (75 ml) malt vinegar
2 tablespoons soft brown sugar
a handful of fresh mint leaves, chopped

BARBECUED FILET MIGNON WITH BÉARNAISE BUTTER

To make the béarnaise butter, beat the butter, garlic, tarragon, and lemon juice in a bowl or food processor until well combined. Place butter onto a sheet of greaseproof paper and roll into a log, using the paper to help you. Refrigerate until set.

Heat the barbecue to medium-high (about 400°F/200°C/gas mark 6) and grease the grill.

Cut the beef into 4 pieces. Grill the beef on the barbecue for 3–4 minutes on each side for medium-rare, or until cooked to your liking. Remove from the grill, cover, and set aside.

Meanwhile, boil the potatoes until just tender, do not let them overcook. Drain the potatoes and leave to stand until dry. Toss the potatoes, mushrooms, oil, salt and pepper together in a bowl. Cook on greased grate of the same barbecue, until browned.

Serve the beef topped with a slice or two of béarnaise butter and accompanied by potato wedges and mushrooms. Remove the cocktail sticks just before serving.

Serves 4

BEARNAISE BUTTER

1 stick (115 g) butter, softened
1 garlic clove, crushed
2 teaspoons finely chopped fresh tarragon
1 tablespoon lemon juice

1 lb 7 oz (650 g) beef eye fillet
4 potatoes, peeled and cut into wedges
14 oz (400 g) brown mushrooms, left whole
2 tablespoons vegetable oil
salt and freshly ground black pepper

SERVING SUGGESTION
Before grilling the beef, wrap 2 slices of prosciutto around each fillet and secure with cocktail sticks. Remove the sticks just before serving.

MUSHROOM STEAK SANDWICH

PLACE THE SALT, PEPPER, AND ROSEMARY in the small bowl of a food processor and mix until finely ground.

Cut the tenderloin crossways into 4 pieces. Gently pound each piece between layers of plastic wrap until about ¼ in/6 mm thick. Rub oil over each steak and sprinkle with the rosemary mixture. Set aside until ready to cook.

Combine the sour cream, horseradish, and mustard in a bowl and set aside.

Melt the butter in a frying pan over a medium-high heat. Add the sliced mushrooms, salt and pepper and fry for about 5 minutes until softened and lightly browned.

Heat the barbecue to medium-high (about 400°F/200°C/gas mark 6) and grease the grill.

Cook the steaks for 2–3 minutes on each side or until cooked to your liking.

Grill the bread, buttered side down, for about 2 minutes until crisp and grill marks appear.

Spread each slice of bread with the sour cream mixture. Make 4 sandwiches with the bread, steak, cheese, and arugula.

SERVES 4

½ teaspoon salt
½ teaspoon freshly ground pepper
1 teaspoon chopped fresh rosemary

1 lb 10 oz (750 g) beef tenderloin
2 teaspoons olive oil
½ cup (115 ml) sour cream
2 tablespoons creamed horseradish
2 teaspoons Dijon mustard
2 tablespoons butter
12 oz (340 g) sliced mushrooms
salt and freshly ground black pepper
8 slices crusty sourdough bread, buttered
8 oz (225 g) Fontina cheese, grated
1 packet of baby arugula leaves

AUSSIE BURGER WITH THE LOT

1 tablespoon vegetable oil
2 onions, thinly sliced
salt and freshly ground black
 pepper
1 lb 4 oz (500 g) minced beef
3 oz (85 g) fine dry breadcrumbs
2 garlic cloves, crushed
2 tablespoons tomato ketchup,
 plus extra for serving
4 slices Cheddar cheese
8 slices smoked streaky bacon
4 pineapple rings
4 burger buns, split
2 teaspoons butter
4 eggs
lettuce leaves, to serve
tomato slices, to serve
8 slices pickled beet, drained,
 to serve

HEAT THE OIL IN A FRYING PAN over a medium heat. Add the onions, salt and pepper and fry for about 15 minutes until browned and softened, stirring occasionally.

Heat a barbecue to medium-high (about 400°F/200°C/gas mark 6) and grease the grill.

Combine the minced beef, breadcrumbs, garlic, ketchup, salt and pepper in a bowl. Shape into 4 patties. Grill on the barbecue for about 4 minutes on each side then set aside and keep warm. Top each hot patty with a slice of cheese.

Grill the bacon on the barbecue for about 4 minutes, or until crisp, and set aside. Grill the pineapple for 3 minutes per side until grill marks appear. Grill the buns for 1 minute until toasted.

Melt the butter in frying pan over a medium heat and fry the eggs in the butter until cooked to your liking.

Place extra ketchup on each bun. Fill with the lettuce, tomato, patty, onions, bacon, pineapple, beet, and top with a fried egg.

SERVES 4

BEEF SALAD WITH THAI DRESSING

To make the dressing, whisk all the ingredients together in a bowl and set aside.

Heat a barbecue to medium-high (about 400°F/200°C/gas mark 6) and grease the grill.

For the beef salad, brush the meat with oil and season with salt and pepper. Grill on the barbecue for 2–3 minutes on all sides until browned. Cover and leave to rest for 5 minutes before cutting into thin slices. Place the slices in a bowl.

Using a vegetable peeler, slice long strips of cucumber and add the slices to the beef. Add the remaining ingredients, drizzle with dressing and toss gently to combine.

Serves 2

THAI DRESSING
1 kaffir lime leaf, finely chopped
2 tablespoons lime juice
1 tablespoon fish sauce
1 tablespoon sugar
1 teaspoon sesame oil
1 teaspoon sambal oelek (chili paste)

BEEF SALAD
4 oz (250 g) beef eye fillet
vegetable oil, for brushing
salt and freshly ground black pepper
1 cucumber
1 small red onion, thinly sliced
a handful of mint leaves
a handful of basil leaves

PANCETTA AND BASIL BEEF BURGER

BASIL MAYONNAISE
½ cup (75 ml) good-quality
  mayonnaise
2 teaspoons Dijon mustard
2 tablespoons chopped fresh basil

PANCETTA AND BASIL BURGERS
1 tablespoon olive oil
2 onions, thinly sliced
salt and freshly ground black
  pepper
1 tablespoon soft brown sugar
8 oz (225 g) fresh breadcrumbs
2 tablespoons milk
1 lb 2 oz (500 g) beef mince
2 garlic cloves, crushed
2 tablespoons Worcestershire
  sauce
2 tablespoons chopped fresh basil
8 slices pancetta
4 crusty bread rolls (such as
  ciabatta) split
a handful of baby spinach leaves

TO MAKE THE BASIL MAYONNAISE, combine all the ingredients in a bowl then set aside in the fridge.

Heat the oil in a frying pan over a medium heat. Add the onions, salt and pepper and fry for about 10 minutes or until golden-brown and softened. Add the sugar and stir until dissolved; set aside to cool slightly.

Combine the breadcrumbs and milk in bowl then set aside for 5 minutes until the milk has been absorbed. Add the beef, garlic, Worcestershire sauce, basil, and a pinch of salt and pepper then mix well to combine. Divide the mixture into four and shape into patties.

Heat the barbecue to medium-high (about 400°F/200°C/gas mark 6) and grease the grill.

Cook the patties on the barbecue for about 5 minutes on each side until cooked through.

Grill the pancetta and buns until slightly crisp and grill marks appear. Top the bottom of each bun with basil mayonnaise, a slice of pancetta, a patty, another slice of pancetta, onions, spinach leaves, and the tops of the buns.

SERVES 4

BALSAMIC BEEF WITH PEPPER AND POTATO SALAD

HEAT THE BARBECUE TO MEDIUM-HIGH (about 400°F/200°C/gas mark 6) and grease the grill.

Place the pepper slices skin side down on the barbecue and grill for about 6 minutes until the skin blisters and blackens. Remove to a bowl, cover and set aside to cool.

Brush the potato slices with oil. Grill on the barbecue for about 3 minutes per side until golden and cooked through, then set aside.

Combine the vinegar, 2 teaspoons of oil, garlic, salt and pepper in a bowl. Reserve half of the mixture in a separate bowl and set aside. Add the steaks to the remaining mixture and toss to cover. Grill on the barbecue for 3–4 minutes on each side for medium-rare. Remove the beef to a plate, cover and leave to rest.

Peel the grilled pepper and cut into thick slices. Add the slices to the reserved balsamic mixture then add the arugula, potatoes, and parsley and gently combine everthing. Serve the salad piled on top of the steaks.

SERVES 2

1 large red pepper, quartered with seeds removed

10 oz (300 g) starchy potatoes thinly sliced

olive oil, for brushing

2 tablespoons balsamic vinegar

2 tablespoons olive oil

1 garlic clove, crushed

salt and freshly ground black pepper

2 x 7 oz (200 g) fillet steaks

a handful of baby arugula leaves

a handful of fresh parsley, coarsely chopped

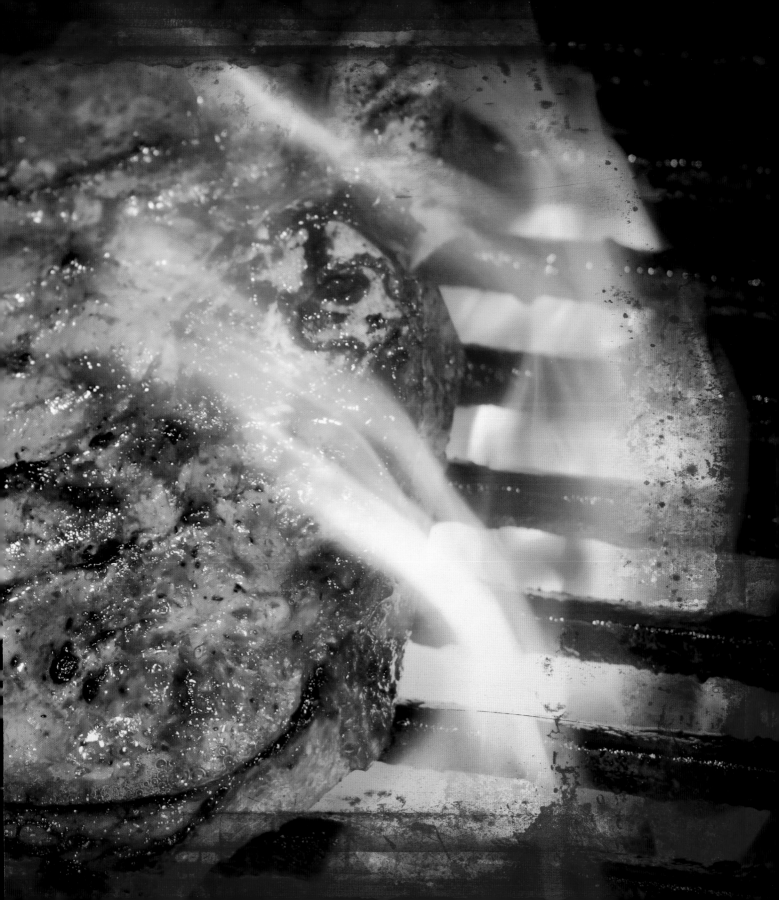

SPICED LAMB AND WATERMELON SALAD

1 tablespoon coarsely chopped rosemary

2 teaspoons cumin seeds

1 teaspoon whole black peppercorns

1 teaspoon dried chili flakes

1 teaspoon salt

1 teaspoon finely grated lemon zest

1 teaspoon finely grated orange zest

¼ cup (55 ml) olive oil

4 x 7 oz (200 g) lamb fillets

½ cup (115 ml) Greek yogurt

a handful of fresh mint, finely chopped

WATERMELON SALAD

1 tablespoon olive oil

1 tablespoon lemon juice

12 oz (350 g) watermelon flesh, chopped

4 oz (125 g) feta cheese, crumbled

2 oz (55 g) kalamata olives, pitted and sliced

POUND THE ROSEMARY, CUMIN, peppercorns, chili, and salt in a mortar and pestle until coarsely ground. Add the lemon and orange zests. Stir in the olive oil. Place the lamb in a shallow dish and rub with the spice mixture. Leave to marinate for at least 1 hour.

Heat the barbecue to medium-high (about 400°F/200°C/gas mark 6) and grease the grill.

Place the lamb on the grill and close the barbecue lid. For medium-rare lamb, cook for 10–12 minutes, turning occasionally. Remove from the grill, cover, and leave to rest for 10 minutes before slicing.

While the lamb is cooking combine the yogurt and mint in a small bowl and set aside.

TO MAKE THE WATERMELON SALAD, whisk the oil and lemon juice in a bowl then add the remaining ingredients and toss to combine. Serve alongside the spiced lamb and the mint dip.

SERVES 4

HONEY-GLAZED LAMB WITH CARROT SALAD

PLACE THE LAMB, CUMIN, CILANTRO, olive oil, honey, and a pinch of salt and pepper in a bowl. Stir gently to completely cover the lamb in the mixture.

Heat the barbecue to medium-high (about 400°F/200°C/gas mark 6) and grease the grill.

Cook the lamb on the barbecue for about 5 minutes per side until cooked to your liking. Remove from the heat, cover and set aside.

TO MAKE THE CARROT SALAD, combine the sesame oil, lime juice, sugar, garlic, and a pinch of salt and pepper in a bowl. Add the remaining ingredients and toss to combine. Serve the carrot salad on top of the lamb.

SERVES 4

12 lamb cutlets, trimmed
1 teaspoon ground cumin
1 teaspoon ground cilantro
1 tablespoon olive oil
1 tablespoon honey
salt and freshly ground black pepper

CARROT SALAD
1 teaspoon sesame oil
2 tablespoons lime juice
1 tablespoon sugar
1 garlic clove, crushed
1 lb 2 oz (500 g) coarsely grated carrot
a handful of cilantro leaves
2 tablespoons toasted sesame seeds

CHILI-CRUSTED BEEF BAVETTE WITH MANGO SALSA

MANGO SALSA

1 red onion, finely chopped

¼ cup (55 ml) lime juice

2 large ripe mangoes, peeled, seeded and chopped

1 red pepper, diced

a handful of fresh cilantro, chopped, plus extra for garnish

1 garlic clove, crushed

¼ cup (55 ml) orange juice

1 jalapeño pepper, finely chopped

salt and freshly ground black pepper

FOR THE BEEF BAVETTE

2 teaspoons ground chili powder

1 teaspoon freshly ground pepper

1 teaspoon ground cumin

½ teaspoon salt

1 lb 10 oz (750 g) beef bavette

TO MAKE THE MANGO SALSA, combine the onion and lime juice in a bowl and leave to stand for 15 minutes. Add the remaining ingredients and stir gently to combine.

Heat the barbecue to medium-high (about 400°F/200°C/gas mark 6) and grease the grill.

FOR THE BEEF, combine the chili powder, pepper, cumin, and salt in a bowl. Rub the mixture over the beef. Grill on the barbecue for 4–6 minutes per side for medium-rare. Cover and allow to rest for 10 minutes before slicing across the grain. Serve topped with the mango salsa and garnish with cilantro leaves.

SERVES 6

PINEAPPLE CHIPOTLE GLAZE STEAK

TO MAKE THE PINEAPPLE CHIPOTLE GLAZE, combine the pineapple juice, orange juice, vinegar and chipotle sauce in a saucepan. Bring the mixture to a boil then reduce the heat to medium and simmer, uncovered, for 10–15 minutes until the mixture has reduced by half. Set aside and leave to cool slightly. Stir in the remaining ingredients.

Heat the barbecue to medium-high (about 400°F/200°C/gas mark 6) and grease the grill.

FOR THE STEAK, combine the cumin, pepper, and salt in bowl then rub the mixture over the beef. Cook the steaks on the barbecue for 4–7 minutes per side depending on their thickness, brushing with the pineapple glaze during cooking. Serve with the grilled pineapple alongside.

SERVES 4

PINEAPPLE CHIPOTLE GLAZE
1 cup (225 ml) pineapple juice
½ cup (115 ml) orange juice
½ cup (115 ml) white wine
  vinegar
1 chipotle pepper in adobo sauce,
  finely chopped
2 tablespoons chopped fresh
  cilantro
1 tablespoon lime juice
salt and freshly ground black
  pepper

FOR THE STEAK
1½ tablespoon ground cumin
1 teaspoon freshly ground pepper
½ teaspoon salt
4 x 7 oz (200 g) boneless beef
  sirloin steaks
4 slices grilled pineapple

PEPPERED STEAK, CAPER, AND POTATO SALAD

1 lb 2 oz (500 g) new potatoes
2 rib steaks, thinly sliced
1 tablespoon olive oil
salt and freshly ground black
  pepper
¼ cup (55 ml) olive oil
2 tablespoons red wine vinegar
2 tablespoons lemon juice
3 tablespoons chopped fresh basil
2 tablespoons capers, coarsely
  chopped
½ teaspoon sugar
1 packet of baby arugula leaves

PLACE THE POTATOES IN A LARGE SAUCEPAN. Cover with water and add a pinch of salt. Cook for about 15 minutes or until tender then drain and leave to cool. When cool enough to handle, cut the potatoes in half then set aside.

Heat the barbecue to medium-high (about 400°F/200°C/gas mark 6) and grease the grill.

Drizzle the beef with oil and season with salt. Generously sprinkle with black pepper. Grill the beef on the barbecue for about 2 minutes until tender.

Whisk the oil, vinegar, lemon juice, basil, capers, sugar, and a pinch of salt and pepper in a large bowl. Add the potatoes, beef, and arugula. Toss gently to combine.

SERVES 4

GRILLED SKIRT STEAK WITH GORGONZOLA SAUCE

COMBINE THE OIL, WINE, WORCESTERSHIRE SAUCE, thyme, garlic, salt and pepper in a bowl. Add the beef and toss to coat. Marinate for at least 1 hour but ideally overnight.

Heat the barbecue to medium-high (about 400°F/200°C/gas mark 6) and grease the grill.

Remove the beef from the marinade. Grill on the barbecue for 4–5 minutes on each side for medium-rare meat. Make sure that you don't overcook the beef as skirt steak can toughen when cooked for too long. Cover and leave to rest for 10 minutes.

Put the cream, Gorgonzola, and horseradish in a saucepan. Stir over a medium-low heat until the cheese has melted then stir in the parsley.

Slice the beef across the grain into thin slices. Serve with the Gorgonzola sauce.

SERVES 6–8

¼ cup (55 ml) olive oil
¼ cup red wine
2 tablespoons Worcestershire sauce
1 tablespoon chopped fresh thyme
4 garlic cloves, crushed
salt and freshly ground black pepper
2 lb 4 oz (1 kg) beef skirt steak
½ cup (115 ml) heavy cream
6 oz (175 g) Gorgonzola cheese
2 teaspoons creamed horseradish
2 tablespoons chopped fresh parsley

HERB-CRUSTED KEBABS WITH TOMATO RELISH

To MAKE THE TOMATO RELISH, combine all the ingredients in a bowl then cover and refrigerate.

To MAKE THE KEBABS, put the herbs, garlic, chili, oil, salt and pepper in a food processor. Mix until finely chopped.

Heat the barbecue to medium-high (about 400°F/200°C/gas mark 6) and grease the grill.

Place the herb mixture and beef cubes into a bowl and stir to coat the meat in the mixture. Thread the coated beef, peppers, and onion alternately onto skewers. Cook the kebabs on the barbecue for about 10 minutes, turning occasionally, or until cooked to your liking. Serve with the tomato relish.

SERVES 6

TOMATO RELISH
2 tomatoes, chopped
¼ cup (55 ml) balsamic vinegar
2 tablespoons olive oil
2 garlic cloves, crushed
2 tablespoons chopped black olives
1 teaspoon sugar
salt and freshly ground black
  pepper

FOR THE KEBABS
a large handful of fresh parsley
a handful of fresh basil leaves
a handful of fresh mint leaves
8 garlic cloves, peeled
1 tablespoon dried chili flakes
⅓ cup (85 ml) olive oil
salt and freshly ground black
  pepper
1 lb 10 oz (750 g) beef sirloin
  steak, cut into 1 in (2.5 cm) cubes
1 medium red pepper, cut into
  1 in (2.5 cm) pieces
1 medium green pepper, cut into
  1 in (2.5 cm) pieces
2 red onions, cut into wedges
12 metal skewers

LAMB AND COLESLAW SLIDERS

To MAKE THE PATTIES, heat the barbecue to medium-high (about 400°F/200°C/gas mark 6) and grease the grill.

Heat the vegetable oil in a medium-sized frying pan. Add the onion, garlic, ginger, salt and pepper. Cook for about 5 minutes until the onion has softened. Combine the minced lamb, onion mixture, breadcrumbs, and hoisin sauce in a medium-sized bowl. Divide the mixture into 12 and shape into patties. Grill the patties on the barbecue for about 5 minutes on each side or until cooked to your liking.

To MAKE THE COLESLAW, stir the honey, soy sauce, vinegar, peanut oil, and sesame oil in medium-sized bowl. Add the remaining ingredients and toss to combine.

Fill the toasted dinner rolls with a patty and coleslaw.

MAKES 12

PATTIES

1 tablespoon vegetable oil
1 onion, finely chopped
2 garlic cloves, crushed
1 tablespoon finely grated ginger
salt and freshly ground black
    pepper
1 lb 2 oz (500 g) lamb mince
3 oz (85 g) fresh breadcrumbs
2 tablespoons hoisin sauce
12 dinner rolls, split and toasted

COLESLAW

1 tablespoon honey
1 tablespoon soy sauce
1 tablespoon rice vinegar
1 tablespoon peanut (or
    vegetable) oil
½ teaspoon sesame oil
4 oz (115 g) grated carrot
12 oz (340 g) finely shredded
    cabbage (preferably Chinese)
a bunch of spring onions, thinly
    sliced

PAPRIKA TARRAGON VEAL CHOPS WITH MUSHROOMS

⅓ cup (85 ml) dry sherry

2 tablespoons vegetable oil

1 tablespoon paprika

1½ teaspoons chopped fresh
tarragon

4 garlic cloves, crushed

salt and freshly ground black
pepper

4 thick veal rib chops

4 portabello mushrooms

4 teaspoons butter

COMBINE THE SHERRY, OIL, PAPRIKA, tarragon, garlic, salt and pepper in a shallow dish. Add the veal and turn to coat it in the mixture. Cover the dish and leave to marinate in the refrigerator for 1–3 hours.

Heat the barbecue to medium-high (about 400°F/200°C/gas mark 6) and grease the grill.

Grill the marinated veal on the barbecue for about 5 minutes on each side until cooked through.

Place the mushrooms cap-side down on the barbecue. Sprinkle with salt and pepper to season then place a teaspoon of butter inside each cap. Cook for 7–10 minutes until the mushrooms have softened. Serve with the veal.

SERVES 4

STEAK WITH GRILLED ONION SALSA

HEAT THE BARBECUE TO MEDIUM (about 350°F/180°C/gas mark 4) and grease the grill.

Cook the onions on the barbecue for about 5 minutes on each side until softened and grill marks appear. Chop the cooked onions and place them into a bowl.

Cook the tomatoes for about 10 minutes, turning occasionally, until the skin begins to char. Chop and add to the onions.

Add the parsley, oregano, vinegar, garlic, 2 tablespoons of oil, salt and pepper. Stir well to combine then leave the bowl in the refrigerator to chill.

Brush extra oil onto the steaks and season with salt and pepper. Grill the steaks on the barbecue for 2–3 minutes on each side until cooked to your liking. Serve with the onion salsa.

SERVES 4

2 large red onions, thickly sliced
2 large vine-ripened tomatoes
1 cup coarsely chopped flat leaf parsley
1 tablespoon chopped fresh oregano leaves
1 tablespoon balsamic vinegar
1 garlic clove, crushed
2 tablespoons olive oil, plus 1 tablespoon extra, for brushing
salt and freshly ground black pepper
4 x 6 oz (175g) beef fillet steaks

MUSTARD AND THYME CRUSTED ROAST BEEF

⅓ cup (85 ml) Dijon mustard
6 garlic cloves, crushed
1½ tablespoon chopped fresh
   thyme
salt and freshly ground black
   pepper
6 lb (2.8 kg) beef sirloin roast
1½ cups (340 ml) red wine
4 oz (115 g) blueberry jam
pinch of ground cinnamon
pinch of cayenne pepper

HEAT THE BARBECUE TO MEDIUM-HIGH (about 400°F/200°C/gas mark 6) and grease the grill.

Combine the mustard, garlic, thyme, salt and pepper in a bowl. Rub the mixture over beef, making sure that every part is covered.

Cook the beef on the barbecue using indirect cooking and with the lid closed for 15 minutes. Reduce the temperature to medium (about 350°F/180°C/gas mark 4). Roast for a further 1 hour or until a meat thermometer registers 149°F/65°C when inserted into the thickest part of the meat (medium-rare).

Cover and leave to rest for 15 minutes before slicing.

Heat the remaining ingredients in a frying pan and season with salt and pepper. Stir the mixture over a medium-high heat until bubbling. Boil, uncovered, for about 5 minutes until the mixture has thickened. Serve with the sliced beef.

SERVES 10–12

BEEF SATAY

To make the peanut sauce, heat the oil in a medium-sized saucepan over a medium heat. Add the shallot, garlic, and chili and cook for 1–2 minutes or until softened and fragrant.

Stir in the remaining ingredients. Cook, uncovered, stirring occasionally, for about 3 minutes or until thickened slightly.

Combine the beef and all the remaining ingredients in a bowl. Cover and marinate in the refrigerator for 1 hour or overnight.

Heat the barbecue to medium-high (about 400°F/200°C/gas mark 6) and grease the grill.

Thread the beef onto 16 metal skewers and grill on the barbecue for about 5 minutes on each side until cooked. Serve with the peanut sauce alongside for dipping.

Makes about 16

PEANUT SAUCE

2 tablespoons peanut (or vegetable) oil
2 tablespoons finely chopped shallot
2 garlic cloves, crushed
1 medium red chili, chopped
1 tablespoon fish sauce
1 tablespoon soy sauce
1 tablespoon lime juice
4 oz (115 g) peanut butter
  (smooth or crunchy)
1 tablespoon soft brown sugar
½ cup (115 ml) coconut milk
  (or water)

BEEF SKEWERS

1 lb 10 oz (750 g) beef sirloin,
  thinly sliced
1 tablespoon finely chopped
  lemongrass
2 oz (55 g) finely chopped shallot
4 garlic cloves, crushed
2 teaspoons finely grated ginger
2 teaspoons ground cilantro
2 teaspoons ground cumin
½ teaspoon turmeric
2 teaspoons soft brown sugar
½ teaspoon salt
2 tablespoons soy sauce
2 tablespoons peanut (or vegetable) oil

LEMON AND HERB ROASTED LAMB

1 tablespoon olive oil

2 tablespoons finely grated lemon zest

8 garlic cloves, crushed

a handful of fresh parsley, chopped

3 tablespoons chopped fresh dill

2 tablespoons chopped fresh oregano

salt and freshly ground black pepper

Approx. 2 lb 4 oz (1 kg) boned lamb leg

pita bread, to serve

hummus, to serve

HEAT THE BARBECUE TO MEDIUM-HIGH (about 450°F/220°C/gas mark 7) and grease the grill.

Combine the oil, lemon zest, garlic, parsley, dill, oregano, salt and pepper in a bowl. Rub the mixture all over the lamb, making sure that every part is covered.

Cook the lamb on the barbecue, using indirect heat and with the lid closed, for about 1 hour, turning once during cooking. Cover and leave to rest for 10 minutes before cutting into thin slices. The lamb should be very tender.

Serve in pita bread with hummus.

SERVES 6

MARMALADE BEER T-BONE STEAKS

WHISK TOGETHER THE BEER, MARMALADE, honey, mustard, ginger, garlic, salt and pepper in a shallow dish. Add the steaks and turn to coat in the marinade. Cover the bowl and refrigerate for 3 hours or overnight.

After marinating, remove the steaks from the bowl and set aside. Pour the marinade into a saucepan and bring to the boil. Allow to boil, uncovered, for 5 minutes.

Heat the barbecue to medium-high (about 400°F/200°C/gas mark 6) and grease the grill.

Season the steaks with salt and pepper. Grill for about 5 minutes on each side, brushing with the warm marinade whilst cooking.

SERVES 4

1½ cups (340 ml) beer
3 oz (85 g) orange marmalade
2 tablespoons honey
1 tablespoon dried mustard
1 tablespoon chopped fresh ginger
4 garlic cloves, crushed
salt and freshly ground black pepper
4 beef T-bone steaks

POULTRY

Chicken is such a versatile meat but we often end up cooking the same old thing. This chapter brings together fresh ideas for chicken on the barbecue, including Sweet Chili Chicken with Avocado Salsa, Garlic Plum Drumsticks, and the ultimate Deluxe Chicken Burger. If you want to be even more adventurous, you'll also find recipes for Roast Goose with Blackberry Port Sauce, Roast Turkey with Hazelnut Stuffing plus a delicious Duck, Orange, and Mint Salad.

LEMON-SPICED CHICKEN WITH APPLE MINT SALSA

HEAT THE BARBECUE TO MEDIUM-HIGH (about 400°F/200°C/gas mark 6) and grease the grill.

Wash the chicken inside and out with cold running water and pat dry with paper towels. Lay breast-side down on a chopping board. Using kitchen scissors, cut down either side of the backbone to remove it. Turn the chicken over and press down lightly to flatten. Carefully run your fingers underneath the skin, loosening it from the flesh across the breast and legs.

Combine the remaining ingredients in a bowl. Spread the mixture evenly in the space you have made between the skin and flesh.

Cook the chicken skin-side up on the barbecue, using indirect heat and with the lid closed, for 1¼–1½ hours, turning during cooking. When the chicken is cooked, the juices will run clear when the thickest part of the thigh is pierced (or a meat thermometer reads 180°F/82°C). Cover the chicken with foil and leave to rest for 10 minutes before carving.

TO MAKE THE APPLE MINT SALSA, heat the oil in a frying pan over a medium-high heat. Add the apples and cook for 3–5 minutes or until lightly browned. Add the sugar and stir until dissolved. Spoon the apples into a bowl and leave to cool slightly. Add the remaining ingredients and stir gently to combine. Serve with the chicken.

SERVES 4

3 lb 12 oz (1.7 kg) whole chicken
8 oz (225 g) softened butter
1 tablespoon finely grated lemon zest
1 teaspoon ground cumin
1 teaspoon crushed dried chilies
2 garlic cloves, crushed
½ teaspoon salt
½ teaspoon freshly ground black pepper

APPLE MINT SALSA
1 tablespoon olive oil
3 green apples, peeled, cored and chopped
2 tablespoons soft brown sugar
salt and freshly ground black pepper
½ teaspoon ground cumin
2 oz (60 g) feta cheese, crumbled
2 tablespoon chopped fresh mint
1 tablespoon lemon juice

SWEET CHILI CHICKEN WITH AVOCADO SALSA AND CORN

AVOCADO SALSA

2 ripe avocados, diced

2 tablespoons lime juice

2 tablespoons chopped fresh
   cilantro

1 garlic clove, crushed

salt and freshly ground black
   pepper

2 tablespoons butter, softened

1 teaspoon finely grated lime zest

salt and freshly ground black
   pepper

4 corn cobs, husks and silk
   removed

4 skinless, boneless chicken
   breasts, sliced in halves horizontally

½ cup (115 ml) sweet chili sauce

To make the salsa, combine all the ingredients in a bowl then set aside to chill in the refrigerator.

Heat the barbecue to medium (about 350°F/180°C/gas mark 4) and grease the grill.

Combine the butter, lime zest, salt and pepper in bowl then brush the mixture over the corn. Cook the corn on the barbecue for about 15 minutes, turn occasionally, until grill marks appear and the kernels are cooked.

Brush the chicken with sweet chili sauce. Grill on the barbecue for about 4 minutes per side until browned and thoroughly cooked through.

Top the chicken with avocado salsa and serve with the grilled corn alongside.

Serves 4

SPICED TURKEY MEATBALLS WITH YOGURT DIPPING SAUCE

To MAKE THE YOGURT DIPPING SAUCE, combine all the ingredients in small bowl.

Heat the barbecue to medium (about 350°F/180°C/gas mark 4) and grease the grill.

Heat the oil in a frying pan over a medium heat. Add the onion and garlic and cook for about 5 minutes or until softened. Add the cumin, pepper, and cinnamon and cook for about 1 minute or until fragrant. Scrape into a bowl.

Add the remaining ingredients to the bowl and mix well to combine. Roll heaped tablespoons of mixture into balls. Grill for 15–20 minutes, turning occasionally, until browned and cooked thoroughly. Serve with the yogurt dipping sauce.

MAKES ABOUT 24 MEATBALLS AND 1 CUP (225 ML) OF SAUCE

YOGURT DIPPING SAUCE

½ cup (150 ml) natural yogurt

1 tablespoon honey

1 tablespoon orange juice

¼ teaspoon freshly ground black
  pepper

salt

FOR THE MEATBALLS

1 tablespoon olive oil

1 onion, finely chopped

2 garlic cloves, crushed

1 teaspoon ground cumin

½ teaspoon freshly ground black
  pepper

¼ teaspoon ground cinnamon

1 lb (500 g) turkey mince

4 oz (115 g) fine breadcrumbs

1 egg, lightly beaten

2 oz (55 g) dried currants

3 oz (85 g) slivered almonds,
  toasted, finely chopped

a large handful of fresh parsley,
  chopped

1 teaspoon grated orange zest

CHICKEN WITH ASPARAGUS AND CHORIZO

HEAT THE BARBECUE TO MEDIUM-HIGH (about 400°F/200°C/gas mark 6) and grease the grill.

Combine 2 teaspoons of oil, the butter, chicken, garlic, salt and pepper in a bowl. Cook the chicken on the barbecue for about 4 minutes on each side or until tender and thoroughly cooked through.

Toss the asparagus in a bowl with the extra oil and season with salt and pepper. Cook on the barbecue for about 5 minutes or until tender on the inside and crisp on the outside. Cook the chorizo slices for 2–3 minutes on each side until browned.

Toss the chicken, asparagus, chorizo, and remaining ingredients in a large bowl and arrange on a platter to serve.

SERVES 6

2 teaspoons olive oil, plus 2 teaspoons extra

2 teaspoons butter, melted

3 skinless, boneless chicken breasts, each cut into 5 strips

4 garlic cloves, crushed

salt and freshly ground black pepper

2 lbs 4oz (1 kg) asparagus, trimmed

2 cooked chorizo sausages, sliced diagonally

4 tomatoes, coarsely chopped

12 black olives, pitted and coarsely chopped

1 tablespoon sweet chilli sauce

2 teaspoons balsamic vinegar

1 x 14fl oz (400 ml) can white beans, (such as cannellini) rinsed and drained

3 oz (85 g) chopped fresh parsley

parmesan shavings, to serve

CHICKEN BURGERS WITH ROASTED PEPPER MAYONNAISE

ROASTED RED PEPPER
MAYONNAISE

2 red peppers, quartered, seeds
    and membranes removed
½ cup (115 ml) good-quality
    mayonnaise
½–1 teaspoon sambal oelek (chili
    paste)
½ teaspoon balsamic vinegar
1 garlic clove, peeled
salt and freshly ground black
    pepper

CHICKEN BURGERS

2 skinless, boneless chicken
    breasts
olive oil
½ teaspoon ground cumin
½ teaspoon dried oregano leaves
4 burger buns, split
2 tomatoes, sliced
mixed baby lettuce leaves
1 red onion, thinly sliced

To make the roasted pepper mayonnaise, heat the barbecue to medium-high (about 400°F/200°C/gas mark 6). Grill the peppers skin-side down for about 5 minutes or until the skin is blistered and blackened. Remove the peppers to a bowl and cover; leave to stand for 10 minutes. Peel away and discard the skin then place the peppers in a blender or food processor.

Add the remaining ingredients and process until smooth.

To make the chicken burgers, place the chicken breasts between layers of plastic wrap. Using the smooth side of a meat mallet or a rolling pin, gently pound the chicken until about **½** in/1 cm thick. Cut both pieces of chicken in half horizontally then brush with a little oil and sprinkle with cumin and oregano. Grill on the barbecue for about 3 minutes on each side or until tender and thoroughly cooked through.

Place the buns cut-side down on the barbecue and grill until golden. Spread both cut sides of each bun with red pepper mayonnaise. Add the grilled chicken, tomato, lettuce, and onion.

Serves 4

ORANGE-SPICED ROAST CHICKEN

3 lb 5 oz (1.5 kg) whole chicken
1 good handful of fresh parsley,
    chopped
1 tablespoon olive oil
2 teaspoons butter, softened
1 tablespoon finely grated orange
    zest
½ teaspoon ground cumin
½ teaspoon ground cilantro
¼ teaspoon ground cinnamon
½ teaspoon sambal oelek (chili
    paste)
salt and freshly ground black
    pepper
2 tablespoons honey

Heat the barbecue to medium-high (about 400°F/200°C/gas mark 6) and grease the grill.

Rinse the chicken inside and out with cold running water and pat dry with paper towels. Lay the chicken breast-side down on a chopping board. Using poultry or kitchen scissors, cut down either side of backbone to remove it (discard the backbone or save it to add to homemade stock). Turn the chicken over and press down lightly to flatten. Carefully run your fingers underneath the skin, loosening it from the flesh across the breast and legs.

Combine the parsley, oil, butter, orange zest, cumin, cilantro, cinnamon, sambal oelek, salt and pepper in a small bowl.

Spread the parsley mixture evenly in the space you have made between the skin and the flesh (because of the chili, it is best to wear a glove for this step).

Cook the chicken, breast-side up, on the barbecue, using indirect heat and with the lid closed for 1¼ hours. Cover chicken the loosely with aluminum foil if it's browning too fast.

Brush the chicken with honey then cook for a further 10 minutes until cooked through. When the chicken is pierced in the thickest part of the thigh the juices should run clear (or a meat thermometer read 180°F/82°C). Allow to rest for 10 minutes before carving.

Serves 4

MUSTARD CHICKEN WITH VEGETABLE PARCELS

COMBINE ALL THE INGREDIENTS, except for the maple syrup, in a bowl or re-sealable plastic bag. Stir or toss to coat chicken in the mixture then cover or seal. Leave to marinate in the refrigerator for about 8 hours or overnight.

TO MAKE THE VEGETABLE PARCELS, heat the barbecue to medium (about 350°F/180°C/gas mark 4) and grease the grill. Cut 4 large sheets of heavy-duty aluminum foil. Spray the foil with cooking spray or grease with a little oil then place the mushrooms and remaining ingredients on each foil sheet. Fold up into parcels and twist to secure.

Grill the chicken on the barbecue, with the lid closed, for 20 minutes, turning occasionally. Brush with maple syrup and cook for a further 5 minutes until the chicken is thoroughly cooked through.

While the chicken is on the barbecue, put the vegetable parcels on the grill and cook for 10–15 minutes until tender.

SERVES 4

3 tablespoons grainy mustard

1 teaspoon grated lemon zest

½ cup (115 ml) lemon juice

1 tablespoon olive oil

1 tablespoon chopped fresh
   rosemary

½ teaspoon freshly ground black
   pepper

2 garlic cloves, crushed

8 chicken drumsticks

8 bone-in chicken thighs

2 tablespoons maple syrup

VEGETABLE PARCELS

4 mushrooms, halved

1 red pepper, seeds and
   membranes removed, sliced

1 small leek, white and tender
   green part only, sliced

12 asparagus spears, chopped

1 garlic clove, crushed

2 teaspoons balsamic vinegar

2 teaspoons olive oil

2 teaspoons maple syrup

salt and freshly ground black
   pepper

BALSAMIC CHICKEN WITH GARLIC HERB POTATOES

COMBINE THE VINEGAR, LEMON ZEST, LEMON JUICE, oil, mustard, salt and pepper in a shallow dish. Add the drumsticks and turn to coat in the mixture. Cover and leave to marinate in the refrigerator for 3 hours or overnight.

Heat the barbecue to medium-high (about 400°F/200°C/gas mark 6) and grease the grill.

Reduce the heat to low and grill the chicken for about 25 minutes, with the lid closed, until thoroughly cooked through. Brush occasionally with the remaining marinade.

TO MAKE THE GARLIC HERB POTATOES, grease a large piece of heavy-duty aluminum foil. Combine all ingredients together on top of the foil. Wrap the foil like a parcel to enclose the potatoes then cook on the barbecue, with the lid closed, for about 45 minutes or until tender, turning occasionally. Serve alongside the chicken.

SERVES 6

½ cup (55 ml) balsamic vinegar

1 tablespoon finely grated lemon zest

3 tablespoons lemon juice

2 tablespoons olive oil

2 tablespoons Dijon mustard

salt and freshly ground black pepper

12 chicken drumsticks, skin removed

GARLIC HERB POTATOES

2 lb 4 oz (1 kg) salad potatoes, quartered

3 tablespoons chopped oregano

1 tablespoon olive oil

½ teaspoon dried chili flakes

3 garlic cloves, crushed

salt and freshly ground black pepper

2 tablespoons lemon juice

DELUXE CHICKEN BURGERS

13 oz (375 g) minced chicken
4 oz (115 g) fine breadcrumbs
2 tablespoons sweet chili sauce
2 garlic cloves, crushed
1 egg, beaten
3 tablespoons chopped parsley
   (or cilantro)
salt and freshly ground black
   pepper
4 pineapple rings
3 oz (85 g) grated Cheddar
3 tablespoons sour cream
3 tablespoons corn relish
4 sesame (or poppy seed) rolls,
   split and buttered
1 avocado, thinly sliced

HEAT THE BARBECUE TO MEDIUM-HIGH (about 400°F/200°C/gas mark 6) and grease the grill. Combine the chicken, breadcrumbs, chili sauce, garlic, egg, and parsley in a bowl and season. Divide the mixture into 4 and shape into patties. Grill the patties for about 5 minutes on each side until cooked through.

Grill the pineapple rings for about 3 minutes on each side until grill marks appear.

Combine the cheese, sour cream, and corn relish in a small bowl. Spread both cut sides of each bun with a dollop of the sour cream mixture. Fill each bun with a patty, a pineapple ring, and a few slices of avocado.

SERVES 4

GINGER, SOY, AND CITRUS CHICKEN

½ cup (55 ml) soy sauce

½ cup (55 ml) rice vinegar

2 tablespoons grated lime zest

1 tablespoon grated ginger

1 tablespoon olive oil

1 tablespoon soft brown sugar

8 bone-in chicken thighs

2 limes, halved

COMBINE THE SOY SAUCE, RICE VINEGAR, lime zest, ginger, oil, and sugar in a shallow dish and mix to combine. Add the chicken and turn to coat in the mixture. Cover the dish and leave to marinate in the refrigerator for 1–3 hours.

Heat the barbecue to medium (about 350°F/180°C/gas mark 4) and grease the grill.

Grill the chicken and limes, cut-side down, on the barbecue for about 10 minutes on each side (for the chicken) until cooked through. Serve half a grilled lime with each serving of chicken.

SERVES 4

POUSSINS WITH PEAR STUFFING

To MAKE THE PEAR STUFFING, heat the oil in a large frying pan over a medium heat. Add the onion and pear and fry for about 5 minutes or until softened. Remove from heat, add the remaining ingredients and mix until well combined.

Heat the barbecue to medium (about 350°F/180°C/gas mark 4) and grease the grill.

Rinse the poussins under cold running water and pat dry inside and out with paper towels. Fill each poussin with about 4 oz (115 g) of stuffing. Season with salt and pepper. Secure the cavity opening with skewers and tie the legs together.

Wrap 2 slices of bacon around each poussin. Cook on the barbecue using indirect heat, for 1–1¼ hours until a meat thermometer registers 170°F /77°C when inserted into the thickest part of the bird. Cover with aluminum foil and allow to rest for 10 minutes before serving.

SERVES 6

PEAR STUFFING

1 tablespoon vegetable oil

8 oz (225 g) finely chopped onion

12 oz (350 g) finely chopped pear

1 lb 2 oz (500 g) fresh fine
  breadcrumbs

8 oz (225 g) walnuts, toasted and
  chopped

2 tablespoons chopped fresh sage

2 teaspoons balsamic vinegar

2 teaspoons soft brown sugar

salt and freshly ground black
  pepper

6 poussins

salt and freshly ground black
  pepper

12 slices streaky bacon

CURRIED CHICKEN SAUSAGES

HEAT THE BARBECUE TO MEDIUM (about 350°F/180°C/gas mark 4) and grease the grill.

Grill the sausages for about 15 minutes, turning occasionally, until cooked and browned. Remove from the grill and slice.

Put the apples and oil in a bowl and stir to coat. Grill on the barbecue for about 10 minutes until softened and grill marks appear. Chop the apple and set aside.

Heat the remaining oil in a frying pan over a medium-high heat. Add the onion and fry, stirring occasionally, for about 10 minutes until softened and lightly browned.

Add the garlic, ginger, and curry powder and fry for about 1 minute or until fragrant, stirring constantly.

Add the stock and bring to the boil. Reduce the heat to medium then add the raisins, apples, sausages, and a pinch of salt and pepper. Cook, uncovered, stirring occasionally, for about 10 minutes or until the sauce has thickened.

SERVES 6

12 good-quality chicken sausages
2 large apples, peeled and
  quartered
2 teaspoons vegetable oil, plus
  1 tablespoon extra
12 oz (350 g) thinly sliced onion
4 garlic cloves, crushed
2 teaspoons grated ginger
2 tablespoons curry powder
2 ⅓ cups (550 ml) chicken stock
8 oz (225 g) dark raisins
salt and freshly ground black
  pepper

SWEET CHICKEN SKEWERS WITH CUCUMBER SALAD

To **MAKE THE CUCUMBER SALAD,** combine the vinegar, water and sugar in a saucepan. Stir over a medium heat until the sugar has dissolved. Simmer for 2 minutes to thicken slightly then remove from the heat and leave to cool completely. Add the remaining ingredients and stir until combined.

To **MAKE THE SWEET CHICKEN SKEWERS**, combine all the ingredients in a bowl. Cover and refrigerate for 30 minutes.

Heat the barbecue to medium (about 350°F/180°C/gas mark 4) and grease the grill. Thread the chicken onto skewers and grill for 10–12 minutes, turning occasionally, until thoroughly cooked. Serve with the cucumber salad.

MAKES 12

CUCUMBER SALAD

½ cup (115 ml) rice vinegar

½ cup (115 ml) water

4 oz (115 g) sugar

2 cucumbers, finely chopped

3 oz (85 g) peanuts, finely chopped

2 tablespoons fish sauce

2 small red chilies, thinly sliced

CHICKEN SKEWERS

a large handful of fresh cilantro, chopped

3 small red chilies, finely chopped

3 tablespoons sugar

3 tablespoons peanut butter

2 tablespoons fish sauce

2 teaspoons lime zest

½ cup (55 ml) lime juice

1 teaspoon ground cumin

4 garlic cloves, crushed

1 lb 10 oz (750 g) skinless, boneless chicken thighs (or breasts), sliced

12 metal skewers

PEPPERED CHICKEN WITH SPICY TOMATO RELISH

SPICY TOMATO RELISH

1 tablespoon olive oil

1 onion, finely chopped

2 garlic cloves, crushed

1 lb 2 oz (500 g) cherry
  tomatoes, halved

4 oz (115 g) sugar

⅓ cup (85 ml) white wine vinegar

½ teaspoon salt

½ teaspoon ground cumin

½ teaspoon dried chili flakes

PEPPERED CHICKEN

4 chicken leg quarters (thigh
  and drumstick attached), skins
  removed

½ teaspoon salt

1 teaspoon freshly ground pepper

To make the spicy tomato relish, heat the oil in a saucepan over a medium heat. Add the onion and garlic. Cook for about 5 minutes or until softened. Add the tomatoes, sugar, vinegar, salt, cumin, and chili. Fry for 10–15 minutes, stirring occasionally, until thickened. Set aside to cool.

Heat the barbecue to high (about 425°F/220°C/gas mark 7) and grease the grill.

Season the chicken with salt and pepper. Reduce the heat to low and grill the chicken for 12–14 minutes on each side until cooked thoroughly. Serve with the tomato relish.

Serves 4

GARLIC PLUM DRUMSTICKS

2 garlic cloves, crushed

2 teaspoons grated ginger

4 oz (115 g) plum jam

a large handful of fresh cilantro, chopped

pinch of Chinese Five-spice powder

2 teaspoons malt vinegar

2 small red chilies, chopped

salt and freshly ground black pepper

8 chicken drumsticks

COMBINE ALL THE INGREDIENTS except the chicken in saucepan. Stir the mixture over a medium heat until the jam has melted.

Heat the barbecue to medium (about 350°F/180°C/gas mark 4) and grease the grill. Reduce the heat to low. Grill the chicken for 20 minutes, turning occasionally. Brush the chicken with the plum jam mixture and grill for a further 10 minutes, brushing frequently, until thoroughly cooked and glazed.

SERVES 4

ROAST GOOSE WITH BLACKBERRY PORT SAUCE

REMOVE THE GIBLETS AND NECK FROM the goose cavity. Rinse inside and out with cold running water.

Half-fill a large saucepan with water and bring to the boil. Wearing clean rubber gloves to protect your hands, place the goose, neck cavity side down, into the boiling water. Hold for 1 minute. Carefully turn the goose and place the other end into the water. Hold for 1 minute. Place the goose on a wire rack over a baking tray and pat dry with paper towel. Allow to stand, uncovered, for 15 minutes or until completely dry.

Heat the barbecue to medium-high (about 400°F/200°C/gas mark 6) and grease the grill.

Season the goose with salt and pepper. Reduce the heat to medium. Cook the goose breast-side down for 1 hour using indirect heat. Turn the goose and cook for another hour or until the skin is browned and a meat thermometer registers 170°F/77°C. Cover and keep warm. Allow to rest for 10 minutes before carving.

To make the blackberry sauce, melt the butter in a frying pan over a medium heat. Add flour and cook for 1 minute. Remove from the heat and gradually stir in the port until smooth. Add the remaining ingredients and stir until well combined. Return to the heat and bring to a boil. Simmer gently, stirring occasionally, for about 10 minutes or until thickened. Strain and serve.

SERVES 6

7 lb (3.6 kg) goose
salt and freshly ground black
  pepper

BLACKBERRY PORT SAUCE
3 tablespoons butter
3 tablespoons plain flour
1 cup (225 ml) port
1 pint (450 ml) chicken stock
3 oz (85 g) blackberry jam
salt and freshly ground black
  pepper

DUCK, ORANGE, AND MINT SALAD

TO MAKE THE HONEY MUSTARD DRESSING, combine all the ingredients in a screw-top jar and shake well.

Score the skin of the duck with a sharp knife. Combine the soy sauce, honey, Chinese Five spice, oil, salt and pepper in bowl. Add the duck, cover and leave to marinate for 1 hour.

Heat the barbecue to medium (about 350°F/180°C/gas mark 4) and grease the grill.

Grill the duck, skin-side down for about 5 minutes or until the skin is crisp. Turn and cook for 3–4 minutes until the skin is crisp and duck is still a little pink inside. Cover and allow to rest for 5 minutes. Cut into thin slices, removing the skin beforehand if preferred.

Bring a saucepan of water to the boil. Add the sugar snap peas and boil for 1 minute or until bright green and crisp. Remove to a bowl of iced water. Leave to stand for 5 minutes then drain.

Toss the duck, peas, and remaining ingredients together in a bowl. Drizzle with the honey mustard dressing and mix gently to combine the flavors.

SERVES 4–6

HONEY MUSTARD DRESSING
3 tablespoons olive oil
2 tablespoons white wine vinegar
½ tablespoon honey
½ tablespoon mustard
½ teaspoon orange zest
salt and freshly ground black
   pepper

FOR THE DUCK
4 x 7 oz (200 g) duck breasts
1 tablespoon soy sauce
1 tablespoon honey
1 teaspoon Chinese Five spice
1 teaspoon olive oil
salt and freshly ground black
   pepper
2 large handfuls of sugar snap
   peas
3 oranges, segmented
a large handful of mint leaves
3 oz (85 g) toasted pumpkin
   seeds

ROAST TURKEY WITH HAZELNUT STUFFING AND ORANGE SAUCE

HAZELNUT AND APRICOT STUFFING

4 slices streaky bacon, finely
   chopped
1 tablespoon butter
1 onion, finely chopped
2 garlic cloves, crushed
1 celery stalk, finely chopped
2 oz (55 g) cranberry jelly
1½ teaspoons finely grated
   orange zest
3 oz (85 g) dried apricots,
   chopped
4 oz (115 g) hazelnuts, toasted,
   peeled and chopped
2 lb (900 g) fresh breadcrumbs
1 apple, peeled and grated
2 teaspoons chopped fresh thyme
salt and freshly ground black
   pepper

FOR THE TURKEY

12 lb (6 kg) turkey, rinsed,
   gizzards and neck removed
2 garlic bulbs, halved
rind of 2 oranges
rind of 2 lemons
4 rosemary sprigs
6 thyme sprigs
¼ stick (55 g) butter, melted
salt and freshly ground pepper

To make the hazelnut and apricot stuffing, fry the bacon in a frying pan over a medium-high heat until browned and crisp. Add the butter, onion, garlic, and celery. Cook, stirring occasionally, for about 5 minutes or until the onion is soft. Add the cranberry jelly and stir until melted.

Combine the onion mixture and remaining stuffing ingredients in a bowl. Spoon the stuffing into the neck cavity and under the skin across the breast and legs of the turkey. Secure with cocktail sticks. Place any remaining stuffing on a greased piece of aluminum foil and fold into a parcel. Cook the parcel with the turkey, using indirect heat, for about 40 minutes, turning occasionally.

Fill the large cavity of the turkey with the garlic, citrus peel, and herbs. Secure any openings with skewers if necessary and tie the legs together. Heat the barbecue to medium-high (about 400°F/200°C/gas mark 6) and grease the grill. Reduce the temperature to medium-low. Season the turkey with salt and pepper and cover loosely with a greased piece of aluminum foil.

Roast for 1¾ hours using indirect heat. Remove the foil and baste with melted butter. Cook for a further 1–1 ½ hours, basting frequently, until the turkey is tender and a meat thermometer inserted into thickest part of leg reads 180°F/82°C. Cover and leave to rest for 15 minutes before carving. Remove the garlic, peel, and herbs from inside the turkey before serving.

To **make the orange brandy sauce,** melt the butter in a saucepan over medium heat. Add the flour and cook for 1 minute. Gradually stir in the brandy then whisk in the remaining ingredients. Allow to simmer for about 10 minutes, stirring occasionally, until the sauce has thickened. Strain if necessary and serve with the turkey and stuffing.

Serves 12

ORANGE BRANDY SAUCE

3 oz (85 g) butter

3 oz (85 g) plain flour

½ cup (115 ml) brandy

2¼ pints (1.3 litres) chicken stock

1 cup (225 ml) orange juice

3 oz (85 g) cranberry jelly

salt and freshly ground black pepper

TAMARIND BARBECUE CHICKEN

HEAT THE BARBECUE TO MEDIUM-LOW (about 325°F/160°C/gas mark 2½) and grease the grill.

Heat the oil in a frying pan over a medium-high heat. Add the onion, garlic, and ginger and cook for about 5 minutes until softened.

Add the ketchup, tamarind, golden syrup, vinegar, mustard, garam masala, salt and pepper. Stir over medium-low heat for 5 minutes until thickened slightly.

Season the chicken with salt and pepper and grill for 15–20 minutes, turning occasionally, until cooked through. Brush liberally with the tamarind sauce and cook for a further 5–7 minutes, basting frequently, until glazed.

MAKES 12

1 tablespoon vegetable oil

1 onion, finely chopped

4 garlic cloves, crushed

2 tablespoons chopped fresh ginger

1 cup (225 ml) tomato ketchup

⅓ cup (85 ml) tamarind purée (or sauce)

⅓ cup (85 ml) golden syrup

¼ cup (55 ml) white vinegar

3 tablespoons wholegrain mustard

1 teaspoon garam masala

salt and freshly ground black pepper

12 chicken drumsticks

BEER-CAN CHICKEN

HEAT THE BARBECUE TO MEDIUM-HIGH (about 400°F/200°C/gas mark 6) and grease the grill.

Rinse the chicken inside and out under cold running water and pat dry with paper towels. Tuck the wings behind then brush the chicken all over with oil.

Combine the mustard, garlic powder, paprika, salt and pepper in a small bowl. Rub the spice mixture all over the chicken and some inside the cavity.

Open the can of beer and pour almost half of the beer out (or drink it!). Place the rosemary sprigs and garlic inside the beer can then place the chicken cavity over the can so it sits comfortably inside the bird.

Cook the chicken on the barbecue using the indirect cooking method for about 1½ hours or until cooked through. When the chicken is pierced in the thickest part of the thigh the juices should run clear (or a meat thermometer read 180°F/82°C). Carefully remove the chicken from the barbecue. Cover with aluminum foil to keep warm and leave to rest for 10 minutes before carving.

SERVES 4

3 ¼ lb (1.7 kg) whole chicken
2 teaspoons olive oil
1 teaspoon dry mustard
1 teaspoon garlic powder
1 teaspoon paprika
¾ teaspoon salt
½ teaspoon freshly ground black pepper
1 can of beer of your choice
2 rosemary sprigs
2 garlic cloves, crushed

PORK

Everyone loves barbecued sausages,
but they can get a bit predictable. In
this chapter you'll find inspiring and
mouthwatering recipes that make the most
of what pork has to offer. Why not try the
Pork and Bacon Skewers with Berry Port
Sauce, or Ginger Pork Chops with Asian
Greens? Get messy with the melt-in-your-
mouth Sticky Spiced Korean Ribs or treat
your friends to Roasted Mustard Pork with
Spinach and Apricot Stuffing. Forget boring
bangers, these recipes will bring your
barbecue cooking to life.

PORK LETTUCE WRAPS

LIME DRESSING
115 ml (4 fl oz) lime juice
115 ml (4 fl oz) fish sauce
3 tablespoons coconut palm sugar
2 tablespoons peanut (or
  vegetable) oil
2 tablespoons kecap manis
  (sweetened, thick soy sauce)
2 garlic cloves, crushed

1 tablespoon finely chopped
  lemongrass (white, tender
  part only)
2 small red chilies, finely chopped
4 garlic cloves, crushed
1 tablespoon finely grated ginger
1 lb 10 oz (750 g) pork steak
1 cucumber, chopped
½ red onion, thinly sliced
4 oz (125 g) bean sprouts
a large handful of mint leaves,
  coarsely chopped
a large handful of cilantro leaves,
  coarsely chopped
lettuce leaves, to serve
chopped toasted peanuts, to serve

TO MAKE THE LIME DRESSING, put all the ingredients in a screw-top jar and shake until well combined.

Mix together the lemongrass, chilies, garlic, ginger, pork, and half of the dressing in a bowl. Cover and marinate for 3 hours or overnight if time permits.

Heat the barbecue to medium-high (about 400°F/200°C/gas mark 6) and grease the grill.

Grill the marinated pork for about 3 minutes on each side or until cooked through. Allow to rest for 5 minutes before cutting into thin strips.

Combine the grilled pork, cucumber, onion, bean sprouts, mint, cilantro, and remaining dressing in a bowl. Arrange on a platter with lettuce leaves and sprinkle with peanuts before serving.

SERVES 6–8

RED PEPPER, GARLIC, AND MOZZARELLA PIZZA

TO MAKE THE RED PEPPER SAUCE, put all the ingredients in a food processor and blend until smooth.

TO MAKE THE PIZZAS, heat the barbecue to high (425°F/220°C/gas mark 7). Spread the red pepper sauce over each pizza base then top with the peppers, garlic, and Parmesan. Reduce the barbecue temperature to medium (about 350°F/180°C/gas mark 4) and grease the grill. Cook the pizzas for about 7 minutes then add the mozzarella and cook for a further 2–3 minutes, or until the base is golden brown and crisp. Remove from the heat.

Arrange the prosciutto, basil, and arugula over each pizza. Drizzle with olive oil and lemon juice and cut into slices before serving.

SERVES 4

ROASTED PEPPER SAUCE
2 roasted red peppers
2 garlic cloves, chopped
1 teaspoon sambal oelek (chili paste)
4 oz (115 g) finely grated fresh Parmesan cheese
salt and freshly ground black pepper
1 teaspoon balsamic vinegar

PIZZA
2 x 12 in /30 cm pre-cooked pizza bases
3 thinly sliced roasted red peppers
4 garlic cloves, crushed
8 oz (225 g) finely grated Parmesan cheese
9 oz (250 g) fresh mozzarella, torn or sliced
7 oz (200g) thinly sliced prosciutto, torn
a handful of basil leaves, torn
2 large handfuls of arugula leaves
olive oil, to serve
fresh lemon juice, to serve

PORK AND BACON SKEWERS

REMOVE ANY FAT FROM THE FILLETS and cut into 1 in/2.5 cm pieces. Combine the vinegar, lemon juice, basil, oil, garlic, salt and pepper in large bowl. Add the pork and stir to combine.

Heat the barbecue to medium (about 350°F/180°C/gas mark 4) and grease the grill.

Cut each slice of bacon into 3 equal pieces. Wrap one slice of bacon around each piece of pork and thread onto metal skewers. Grill on the barbecue for about 15 minutes, turning occasionally, until cooked through. Be careful to not overcook the pork.

TO MAKE THE BERRY AND PORT SAUCE, melt the butter in a large frying pan over a medium-high heat. Add the shallots and cook for about 3 minutes or until softened. Add the remaining ingredients and cook for about 10 minutes, stirring occasionally, or until the sauce has thickened. Serve with the pork skewers.

SERVES 4–6

1 lb 10 oz (750 g) pork fillets
2 tablespoons balsamic vinegar
2 tablespoons lemon juice
2 tablespoons chopped fresh basil
1 tablespoon olive oil
6 garlic cloves, crushed
1 teaspoon salt
1 teaspoon freshly ground black
    pepper
12 slices streaky bacon
6–8 metal skewers

BERRY PORT SAUCE
1 tablespoon butter
2 oz (55 g) chopped shallots
⅓ cup (85 ml) port
1½ cups (340 ml) chicken stock
1 punnet of blueberries
salt and freshly ground black
    pepper

ROASTED MUSTARD PORK WITH SPINACH AND APRICOT STUFFING

1 tablespoon olive oil
1 onion, finely chopped
12 oz (340 g) spinach, coarsely chopped
4 oz (115 g) walnuts, toasted and chopped
4 oz (115 g) dried apricots, finely chopped
1 apple, peeled and grated
12 oz (340 g) fresh breadcrumbs
2 tablespoons chopped fresh parsley
salt and freshly ground black pepper
5 lb (2.25 kg) boneless pork loin
2 tablespoons wholegrain mustard

APPLE MUSTARD GRAVY
2 tablespoons butter
2 tablespoons plain flour
1 pint (500 ml) chicken stock
6 tablespoons apple sauce
1 tablespoon wholegrain mustard
salt and freshly ground black pepper

HEAT THE OIL IN A FRYING PAN OVER A MEDIUM-HIGH HEAT. Add the onion and fry, stirring occasionally, for about 5 minutes or until softened. Add the spinach and stir until just wilted. Spoon into a bowl then add the walnuts, apricots, apple, breadcrumbs, parsley, salt and pepper. Mix to combine.

Heat the barbecue to medium-high (about 400°F/200°C/gas mark 6) and grease the grill.

Cut a large slit in the pork horizontally, starting and finishing about ½ in/1 cm from each end and being careful to not cut all the way through to the other side. Fill the opening with the spinach stuffing and secure with metal skewers or tie with string. Rub the pork all over with mustard and season with salt and pepper. Cook the pork on the barbecue using the indirect cooking method and with the lid closed for 1–1¼ hours, turning occasionally, until cooked. Cover and leave to rest for 10 minutes before carving into thick slices.

TO MAKE THE APPLE MUSTARD GRAVY, melt the butter in a frying pan over a medium heat. Stir in the flour and cook for 1 minute. Gradually stir in the stock. Bring the mixture to the boil then stir in the apple sauce, mustard, salt and pepper. Reduce the heat to medium-low and simmer, uncovered, for about 10 minutes or until thickened. Serve with the pork.

Serves **10**

STICKY SPICED KOREAN RIBS

½ cup (115 ml) sweet chili sauce
⅓ cup (85 ml) lime juice
3 tablespoons melted butter
2 teaspoons ground cumin
2 teaspoons garlic powder
salt, to taste
1 teaspoon cracked black pepper
2 lbs (1 kg) Korean short ribs

COMBINE THE SWEET CHILI SAUCE, LIME JUICE, butter, cumin, garlic powder, salt and pepper in a bowl.

Heat the barbecue to medium (about 350°F/180°C/gas mark 4) and grease the grill.

Cook the ribs on the barbecue for 10–15 minutes, brushing with the sweet chili mixture occasionally, until cooked through and glazed.

SERVES 4

PORK, LENTIL, AND CUCUMBER WRAPS

To MAKE THE LENTIL AND CUCUMBER SALAD, mix together all the ingredients in a medium-sized bowl. Cover and set aside in the refrigerator.

Cut the pork horizontally into thin slices. Place the slices in a glass bowl and add the oil, cumin, sugar, chilies, lemon zest, garlic, yogurt, and a generous pinch of salt and pepper. Cover and chill for 3 hours or overnight.

Heat a grill or barbecue to medium-high (about 400°F/200°C/gas mark 6). Cook the pork for 2–3 minutes on each side or until tender and cooked through.

Spread the pita breads with red pepper jelly then spoon the salad and pork into the pittas, ready to serve.

MAKES 6

LENTIL AND CUCUMBER SALAD
½ cup (115 ml) natural yogurt
3 tablespoons lemon juice
1 x 14 oz (400 g) can lentils,
   rinsed and drained
1 cucumber, halved lengthways
   and thinly sliced
4 spring onions, thinly sliced
2 tablespoons chopped fresh
   cilantro (or mint)
2 garlic cloves, crushed
salt and freshly ground black
   pepper

1 lb 6 oz (625 g) pork fillet
1 tablespoon olive oil
2 teaspoons ground cumin
1 tablespoon soft brown sugar
2 teaspoons dried chili flakes
2 teaspoons finely grated
   lemon zest
4 garlic cloves, crushed
½ cup (115 ml) natural yogurt
salt and freshly ground black
   pepper
6 small pita breads, warmed
2 oz (55 g) red pepper jelly

ROASTED SPICED PORK PITAS WITH TOMATO AND MINT SALAD

COMBINE THE HONEY, OIL, LEMON ZEST, cumin, chilies, garlic, and a pinch of salt and pepper in a medium-sized dish. Add the pork and turn to coat in the mixture. Cover and marinate in the refrigerator for 1 hour or ideally overnight.

Remove the pork from the refrigerator and leave to stand for 30 minutes at room temperature before roasting.

Heat the barbecue to medium-high (about 400°F/200°C/gas mark 6) and grease the grill.

Cook the pork on the barbecue, using the indirect cooking method and with the lid closed, for 1–1¼ hours, turning occasionally, until cooked. Cover and allow to rest for 10 minutes before carving into thin slices. Cut each slice in half.

TO MAKE THE TOMATO SALAD, combine all the ingredients in a medium-sized bowl.

Heat the pita breads on the barbecue until warmed. Spread with yogurt then top with the pork and tomato salad. Drizzle with oil and serve with lemon wedges.

SERVES 6

2 tablespoons honey
1 tablespoon olive oil
1 tablespoon finely grated lemon zest
2 teaspoons ground cumin
1 teaspoon crushed dried chilies
4 garlic cloves, crushed
salt and freshly ground black pepper
2 lb 4 oz (1 kg) boneless pork loin
8 pita breads
1 cup (225 ml) Greek yogurt

TOMATO SALAD
4 large tomatoes, chopped
1 x 14 oz (400 g) can chickpeas, rinsed and drained
1 red onion, thinly sliced
a handful of chopped fresh mint leaves
2 tablespoons lemon juice
1 teaspoon ground cumin
salt and freshly ground black pepper
olive oil, to serve
lemon wedges, to serve

GINGER PORK CHOPS WITH ASIAN GREENS

⅓ cup (85 ml) oyster sauce
⅓ cup (85 ml) soy sauce
2 tablespoons finely grated ginger
2 tablespoons honey
3 garlic cloves, crushed
1 tablespoon vegetable oil
4 x 7 oz (200 g) pork chops
1 bunch baby pak choi, quartered
    (or 2 bunches baby pak choi,
    halved)
chili sauce, to serve

COMBINE THE OYSTER SAUCE, SOY SAUCE, ginger, honey, garlic, and oil in a shallow dish. Add the pork chops and turn to coat.

Heat the barbecue to medium-high (about 400°F/200°C/gas mark 6) and grease the grill.

Cook the chops on the barbecue about 5 minutes on each side, depending on the thickness.

Cook the pak choi on the barbecue for about 3 minutes on each side until tender but retaining a little crunch. Remove from the barbecue and coarsely chop. Serve with the pork chops and chili sauce.

SERVES 4

PORK AND SHRIMP PATTIES

2 garlic cloves, peeled
1 tablespoon chopped ginger
1 tablespoon soft brown sugar
2 tablespoons cilantro leaves
1 small red chili
2 teaspoons fish sauce
1 egg white
10½ oz (300 g) cooked, peeled shrimp, veins removed
5½ oz (150 g) pork mince
4 lettuce leaves, to serve
sweet chili sauce, to serve

HEAT THE BARBECUE TO MEDIUM (about 350°F/180°C/gas mark 4) and grease the grill.

Put the garlic, ginger, sugar, cilantro, chili, fish sauce, and egg white in a food processor and mix until combined. Add the shrimp and pork. Process until well combined and the shrimp are finely chopped.

Divide the mixture into 8–10 portions and shape into patties. Grill the patties on the barbecue for about 4 minutes on each side or until cooked.

Place 2 patties on each lettuce leaf. Drizzle with sweet chili sauce before serving.

SERVES 2–4

CARAMEL BALSAMIC PORK BELLY

HEAT THE BARBECUE TO MEDIUM-LOW, (about 325°F/160°C/gas mark 2½) and grease the grill.

Cut the pork into even-sized pieces. Thread the pieces onto metal skewers place in a disposable foil dish.

Combine the sugar, water, vinegar, garlic, salt and pepper in a bowl. Stir until sugar is dissolved then pour over the pork. Cover with aluminum foil and cook on the barbecue using the indirect cooking method for 30 minutes. Turn the pork and remove the foil. Increase the heat to medium-high (about 400°F/200°C/gas mark 6). Cook for a further 30–45 minutes, turning occasionally, or until caramelized, being careful not to burn the sauce.

Brush the cut side of each fig with honey. Cook on the barbecue over a medium direct heat for 1–2 minutes or until softened and grill marks appear. Serve the figs with the pork skewers.

SERVES 4

2 lb 4 oz (1 kg) pork belly, skin removed
8 oz (225 g) soft brown sugar
1 cup (225 ml) water
⅓ cup (85 ml) balsamic vinegar
2 garlic cloves, crushed
salt and freshly ground black pepper
8 figs, halved
2 tablespoons honey

VIETNAMESE-STYLE PORK BUNS

2 oz (55 g) caster sugar

1 tablespoon fish sauce

1 garlic clove, crushed

2 teaspoons sesame oil

14 oz (400 g) pork fillet, trimmed and halved lengthwise

1 baguette, split and quartered

½ cup (55 g) good-quality mayonnaise

SALAD

2 tablespoons lime juice

1 tablespoon fish sauce

1 tablespoon sugar

1 teaspoon sesame oil

1 red onion, thinly sliced

4 oz (115 g) grated carrot

½ cucumber, thinly sliced

2 tablespoons coarsely chopped cilantro

2 tablespoons coarsely chopped mint leaves

HEAT THE BARBECUE TO MEDIUM (about 350°F/180°C/gas mark 4) and grease the grill.

Combine the sugar, sauce, garlic, and oil in bowl. Add the pork and stir to coat. Cook the pork on the barbecue, turning occasionally, for 10–15 minutes or until just cooked through. Allow to rest for 10 minutes before cutting into thin slices.

Spread each piece of baguette with mayonnaise and add a few slices of pork.

TO MAKE THE SALAD, combine all the ingredients in a bowl and toss to coat. Top each baguette with salad.

SERVES 4

CURRIED PORK AND MANGO WRAP

7 oz (200 g) pork fillet
oil, for brushing
salt and freshly ground black
  pepper
2 tablespoons good-quality
  mayonnaise
½ teaspoon curry powder
2 large flour tortillas
2 tablespoons mango chutney
6 oz (175 g) finely shredded red
  cabbage
6 oz (175 g) finely shredded
  romaine lettuce
2 oz (55 g) thinly sliced celery
3 oz (85 g) sliced fresh mango
  (or canned, drained well)
2 tablespoons thinly sliced
  spring onions
2 oz (55 g) sliced almonds,
  toasted

HEAT THE BARBECUE TO MEDIUM-HIGH (about 400°F/200°C/gas mark 6) and grease the grill.

Brush the pork fillet with oil and season with salt and pepper. Cook on the barbecue, turning occasionally, for 10–12 minutes or until tender and grill marks appear. Allow to rest for 5 minutes before cutting into thin slices or shredding.

Combine the mayonnaise and curry powder in a bowl. Spread over one half of both tortillas then spread other half with mango chutney.

Lay the pork and all the remaining ingredients down the center of each tortilla, then roll up firmly to enclose the filling.

MAKES 2

ASPARAGUS, PORK, AND HALLOUMI STACKS

COMBINE THE OIL, GARLIC, MINT, ORANGE JUICE, harissa, cumin, salt and pepper in a bowl.

Place the pork between layers of plastic wrap. Using a rolling pin, gently pound the pork until about ¼ in/5 mm thick. Add the pork to the oil mixture and turn to coat. Cover and refrigerate for 30 minutes or ideally overnight.

Heat the barbecue to medium (about 350°F/180°C/gas mark 4) and grease the grill.

Remove the pork from the marinade and pat dry with paper towels. Grill for 2–3 minutes on each side until cooked through and grill marks appear. Cover and set aside for 5 minutes to rest.

Meanwhile, brush the asparagus with a little oil and grill on the barbecue for 5–6 minutes, turning occasionally until tender but still with a little crunch.

Brush the halloumi with a little oil. Grill for about 2 minutes on each side or until grill marks appear. Serve the pork with the halloumi stacked on top, then the asparagus. Sprinkle with Parmesan and serve with lemon wedges.

SERVES 4

1 tablespoon olive oil, plus extra
   for brushing
4 garlic cloves, crushed
3 oz (85 g) chopped fresh mint
⅓ cup (85 ml) orange juice
1 tablespoon harissa
1 teaspoon ground cumin
salt and freshly ground black
   pepper
4 x 15 oz (225 g) pork escallopes
1 bunch asparagus, trimmed
6 oz (175 g) halloumi cheese
2 oz (55 g) finely grated fresh
   Parmesan cheese
lemon wedges, to serve

GRILLED VEGETABLE, BACON, AND GOATS' CHEESE BRUSCHETTA

2 tablespoons balsamic vinegar

2 tablespoons lemon juice

2 tablespoons olive oil, plus
1 teaspoon extra for brushing

salt and freshly ground black
pepper

1 zucchini, thinly sliced
lengthways

1 eggplant, thinly sliced
lengthways

1 lb 2 oz (500 g) asparagus
spears, trimmed

8 spring onions, trimmed

8 streaky bacon slices

1 ciabatta loaf, cut into ¼ in/6 mm
-thick slices

10 oz (280 g) goats' cheese,
softened

3 tablespoons finely chopped
fresh basil

1 teaspoon ground cumin

HEAT THE BARBECUE TO MEDIUM-HIGH (about 400°F/200°C/gas mark 6) and grease the grill.

Combine the vinegar, lemon juice, 2 tablespoons of oil, salt and pepper in a large, shallow dish. Add the zucchini, eggplant, asparagus, and spring onions and toss until coated.

Remove the vegetables from the marinade, reserving any leftover marinade. Grill the vegetables and bacon on the barbecue, turning occasionally, for 3–4 minutes or until tender and grill marks appear. Finely chop the vegetables and bacon and set aside in a bowl with the reserved marinade.

Brush the bread with extra oil and grill for about 1 minute on each side or until grill marks appear.

Combine the goats' cheese, basil, and cumin in a bowl then spread onto each slice of bread. Top with the bacon and vegetable mixture. Serve warm.

SERVES 4

PESTO PORK MEATBALLS

1 lb 2 oz (500 g) pork mince
2 large onions, finely chopped
4 garlic cloves, crushed
12 oz (340 g) fresh breadcrumbs
3 tablespoons basil pesto
a handful of fresh parsley, chopped
3 oz (85 g) pine nuts, toasted
3 oz (85 g) fresh Parmesan cheese, finely grated
1 egg, lightly beaten
salt and freshly ground black pepper
2 tablespoons Worcestershire sauce
2 tablespoons tomato purée

COMBINE THE PORK MINCE, ONIONS, garlic, breadcrumbs, pesto, parsley, pine nuts, cheese, egg, salt and pepper in a bowl. Scoop up heaped tablespoons of mixture and shape into balls; flatten slightly.

Heat the barbecue to medium-low (about 325°F/160°C/gas mark 2½) and grease the grill.

Cook the meatballs on the barbecue with the lid closed for 10 minutes, turning occasionally.

Combine the Worcestershire sauce and tomato purée in a bowl. Add the meatballs and turn to coat in the mixture. Cook the coated meatballs for about 5 minutes, turning occasionally, until cooked through.

SERVES 3–4

SWEET CHILI PORK WITH CRISPY WONTONS

DEEP-FRY THE WONTONS IN A LARGE PAN until lightly golden. Remove with a slotted spoon and drain on paper towel. Be careful as the oil will be very hot.

Heat the barbecue to medium (about 350°F/180°C/gas mark 4) and grease the grill.

Combine the chili sauce, ginger, garlic, and soy in a bowl. Reserve and set aside half of the mixture.

Place the pork between layers of plastic wrap. Using a rolling pin, pound until ¼ in /6 mm thick. Stir together the pork, 1 tablespoon oil, salt, pepper and half of the chili sauce mixture in a bowl. Cook on the barbecue for 2–3 minutes until cooked and browned. Cut the pork into strips.

Toss together the hot pork, cucumber and the reserved chili sauce mixture in bowl. Serve with crispy wontons.

SERVES 4

8 wonton wrappers, halved diagonally
vegetable oil for deep-frying, plus 1 tablespoon extra
¾ cup (175 ml) sweet chili sauce
2 teaspoons finely grated ginger
4 garlic cloves, crushed
2 teaspoons soy sauce
4 pork steaks
salt and freshly ground black pepper
1 cucumber, chopped

BROWN SUGAR AND BEER RIBS

2 lb 4 oz–3 lb (1–1.3 kg) pork loin back ribs
1 tablespoon olive oil
4 garlic cloves, crushed
salt and freshly ground black pepper
¼ cup (55 ml) beer
¼ cup (55 ml) barbecue sauce
2 tablespoons Dijon mustard
2 tablespoons brown sugar
2 tablespoons Worcestershire sauce

HEAT THE BARBECUE TO MEDIUM-HIGH (about 400°F/200°C/gas mark 6) and grease the grill.

Rub the ribs with oil and season generously with salt and pepper.

Using the indirect cooking method, grill the ribs for 45 minutes, turning occasionally. Turn the heat to low (about 275°F/140°C/gas mark 1) then cook for a further 15 minutes, frequently basting the ribs with the beer mixture, until cooked through and grill marks appear. Cut the ribs into sections before serving.

SERVES 2–3

FISH & SEAFOOD

Fish can sometimes be a hard-sell at barbecues, with everyone diving for the more meaty options. This chapter will show you just how exciting and varied barbecued fish can be and will have even the most ardent fish-avoiders tucking in. Fresh, light, and healthy, these recipes are perfect for hot summer days and range from Grilled Lemongrass Shrimp and Miso Sesame Salmon to Coconut Grilled Bream and Mussels in White Wine, Basil, and Chili. Delicious!

LEMONGRASS SHRIMP

PEEL AND DEVEIN THE SHRIMP, leaving the heads and tails intact.

Combine the chilies, garlic, lemongrass, soy sauce, oil, and sugar in a bowl. Add the shrimp and stir to coat. Cover and place in the refrigerator for 1 hour.

Heat the barbecue to medium (about 350°F/180°C/gas mark 4) and grease the grill.

Thread the shrimp lengthways onto metal skewers, allowing one prawn per skewer. Grill on the barbecue for 2–3 minutes per side or until the shrimp are cooked through. Serve with lime wedges.

SERVES 4

2 lbs (1kg) medium-large raw shrimp
2 small red chilies, finely chopped
4 garlic cloves, crushed
1 stalk lemongrass, white part only, finely chopped
3 tablespoons soy sauce
2 tablespoons vegetable oil
1 tablespoon sugar
1 lime, quartered, to serve

FISH AND COLESLAW TACOS

COLESLAW

½ cup (55 ml) mayonnaise

1 tablespoon white vinegar

1 tablespoon sugar

salt and freshly ground black pepper

8 oz (225 g) finely shredded cabbage

2 tablespoons olive oil

1 teaspoon dried chili flakes

½ teaspoon salt

4 snapper fillets (about 1 lb 2 oz/ 500 g in total)

1 red onion, thinly sliced

1 ripe avocado, sliced

4 flour tortillas

a handful of fresh cilantro, to garnish

To make the coleslaw, combine all the ingredients in a bowl. Cover and refrigerate until ready to use.

Combine the oil, chili flakes, and salt in a bowl then brush over the fish. Heat the barbecue to medium (about 350°F/180°C/gas mark 4). Grease a large piece of heavy-duty aluminum foil. Poke holes in the foil using a skewer then place on the barbecue grill. Place the fish on top of the foil and close the barbecue lid. Cook for about 6 minutes, depending on the thickness of the fish, or until just cooked. Place the fish in a clean bowl and flake with a fork.

Place portions of fish, onion, avocado, and coleslaw on each tortilla and fold in half to make a taco. Garnish with cilantro.

Serves 4

LEMON FISH AND CHIPS

1 teaspoon finely grated
  lemon zest
1 teaspoon salt
4 sea bass fillets
  (7 oz/200 g each)
2 tablespoons melted butter
hot, oven-roasted chips, to serve

HEAT THE BARBECUE TO MEDIUM (about 350°F/180°C/gas mark 4) and grease the grill.

Place the lemon zest and salt in a small processor, such as a spice grinder. Process until well combined.

Brush the fillets with the melted butter. Cook the on the barbecue for 3–4 minutes on each side, depending on the thickness of the fillets. Brush frequently with butter and be careful to not overcook the fish.

Sprinkle the fish and chips with the lemon and salt mixture before serving.

SERVES 4

SCALLOP AND SHRIMP SALAD WITH GINGER DRESSING

TO MAKE THE GINGER DRESSING, place all the ingredients in a screw-top jar and shake until well combined.

Heat the barbecue to medium-high (about 400°F/200°C/gas mark 6) and grease the grill.

Lightly stir together the oil, scallops, shrimp, salt and pepper in a bowl. Grill on the barbecue for 2–3 minutes per side until just cooked. Remove to a bowl and set aside to cool.

Add the onions, cilantro, chilies, arugula, and dressing to the bowl and toss to combine. Add the noodles just before serving.

SERVES 4–6

GINGER DRESSING

1 tablespoon finely grated ginger
½ cup (55 ml) peanut (or
    vegetable) oil
2 garlic cloves, crushed
2 tablespoons rice vinegar
2 tablespoons lime juice
2 tablespoons soy sauce
1 tablespoon sugar
salt and freshly ground black
    pepper

1 tablespoon peanut (or
    vegetable) oil
1 lb 2 oz (500 g) large scallops
1 lb 5 oz (600 g) large, raw
    shrimp, peeled and deveined
    with tails intact
salt and freshly ground black
    pepper
1 bunch spring onions, thinly
    sliced
a handful of fresh cilantro
2–3 small red chilies, thinly
    sliced
arugula (or baby salad leaves),
    to serve
2 cups crunchy noodles

MISO SESAME SALMON

Heat the barbecue to medium (about 350°F/180°C/gas mark 4) and grease the grill.

Slice the salmon into 4 equal pieces.

Combine the miso, vinegar, sugar and oil in a bowl. Add the salmon and stir carefully to coat. Cook the salmon skin side down on the barbecue for about 5 minutes or until the skin is crisp. Turn over and cook for a further 2 minutes until just cooked.

To cook the garlic sugar snap peas, heat a wok over a high heat. Add the oil and garlic and stir for 30 seconds. Add the peas and stir-fry for about 2 minutes or until tender but still with a little bite.

Serve the salmon and peas sprinkled with sesame seeds.

Serves 4

650 g (1 lb 7 oz) salmon, skin on, pin bones removed
2 tablespoons white miso paste
2 tablespoons rice wine vinegar
2 teaspoons sugar
1 teaspoon sesame seed oil
2 tablespoons sesame seeds, toasted

GARLIC SUGAR SNAP PEAS
2 teaspoons sesame seed oil
2 garlic cloves, sliced
400 g (14 oz) sugar snap peas, trimmed
salt and freshly ground black pepper

TUNA BEAN SALAD WITH OLIVE DRESSING

OLIVE DRESSING

2 oz (55 g) olives, pitted

½ cup (55 ml) olive oil

2 tablespoons red wine vinegar

1 garlic clove, peeled

FOR THE SALAD

1 lb 5 oz (600 g) tuna steak

vegetable oil, for brushing

salt and freshly ground black pepper

1 x 14 oz (400 g) can white beans (such as cannellini), rinsed and drained

1 roasted red pepper, thinly sliced

a handful of fresh parsley, chopped

1 red onion, chopped

2 tablespoons capers, drained

TO MAKE THE OLIVE DRESSING, place all the ingredients in a food processor and blend until smooth.

Heat a barbecue to medium-high (about 400°F/200°C/gas mark 6) and grease the grill.

Brush the tuna with oil and season with salt and pepper. Cook on the barbecue for 2–3 minutes on each side until grill marks appear but the tuna is still a little pink inside. Remove from the heat and break apart with a fork. Gently mix together the tuna, dressing, and remaining ingredients in a bowl.

SERVES 4

COCONUT GRILLED BREAM

8 oz (225 g) cooked jasmine rice

⅓ cup (85 ml) coconut milk

2 tablespoons chopped fresh
  cilantro

1 teaspoon finely grated ginger

1 small red chili, finely chopped

salt, to taste

2 x sea bream (or snapper),
  gutted and cleaned
  (10 oz/300 g each)

2 tablespoons soy sauce

1 tablespoon honey

cilantro leaves, to serve

lime wedges, to serve

HEAT THE BARBECUE TO MEDIUM (about 350°F/180°C/gas mark 4) and grease the grill.

Combine the rice, coconut milk, cilantro, ginger, chili, and salt in a bowl. Place half of the mixture in the cavity of each fish. Secure any openings with small metal skewers.

Combine the soy sauce and honey in bowl and brush a little onto the fish. Cook on the barbecue for 7–10 minutes on each side, basting with soy mixture but keeping the lid closed as much as possible. Serve sprinkled with cilantro leaves and lime wedges.

SERVES 4

GRILLED BASIL TROUT WITH WINE SAUCE

HEAT THE BARBECUE TO MEDIUM-HIGH (about 400°F/200°C/gas mark 6) and grease the grill.

Place 2 sprigs of basil inside each trout then season with salt and pepper. Cook on the barbecue with the lid closed for 6–10 minutes per side or until cooked.

Meanwhile, melt the butter in a frying pan over a medium heat. Add the onion and garlic and cook for about 5 minutes or until the onion has softened.

Stir in the wine, sambal oelek, salt and pepper. Boil gently, uncovered, for about 3 minutes or until the mixture has reduced by half. Stir in the cream and reduce the heat to medium. Simmer for about 3 minutes. Stir in the chopped basil.

Pour the sauce over the trout before serving.

SERVES 2

4 sprigs basil, plus 2 tablespoons finely chopped basil leaves
2 trout (10½ oz/300 g), cleaned and gutted
salt and freshly ground black pepper
2 tablespoons butter
1 large onion, finely chopped
4 garlic cloves, minced
1 cup (225 ml) dry white wine
1 teaspoon sambal oelek (chili paste)
½ cup (115 ml) heavy cream

MUSSELS IN WHITE WINE, BASIL, AND CHILI

HEAT THE BARBECUE TO MEDIUM-HIGH (about 400°F/200°C/gas mark 6).

Combine all the ingredients in a large bowl. Spread a large piece of heavy-duty aluminum foil on the work surface. Pile the mussels onto the foil then bring the sides up and over to form a parcel. Wrap a second piece of foil around the first.

Cook the mussels on the barbecue, with the lid closed, for 7–10 minutes until just cooked. Discard any unopened mussels before serving.

SERVES 4–6

2 tablespoons butter, melted
2 garlic cloves, minced
½ cup (115 ml) dry white wine
1 teaspoon sambal oelek
   (chili paste)
½ cup (115 ml) heavy cream
3 lb 5 oz (1.5 kg) mussels,
   cleaned and beards removed
3 tablespoons chopped fresh basil
salt and freshly ground black
   pepper

BAKED FISH WITH CHILI AND LIME

HEAT THE BARBECUE TO HIGH (about 425°F/220°C/gas mark 7).

Lay 4 pieces of aluminum foil on the work surface and grease. Taking half of the lime slices, divide evenly into 4 and place in the center of each piece of foil. Sprinkle with half of the chilies, garlic, and cilantro then top with a fish fillet. Arrange the remaining lime slices, chilies, garlic and coriander over top of the fish.

Combine the soy sauce, honey, salt and pepper in a bowl and drizzle over the fish. Wrap the foil around the fish to form a parcel. Turn the barbecue down to medium-low (about 350°F/180°C). Cook the fish for about 15 minutes or until just cooked and it can be flaked with a fork.

SERVES 4

3–4 limes, thinly sliced
6 small red chilies, chopped
4 garlic cloves, crushed
a good handful of fresh cilantro
  leaves
4 halibut steaks or fillets
  (about 1 lb 12 oz /800 g total
  weight)
⅓ cup (55 ml) soy sauce
⅓ cup (55 ml) honey
salt and freshly ground black
  pepper

THAI FISH CAKES

DIPPING SAUCE

⅓ cup (85 ml) rice vinegar

⅓ cup (85 ml) water

3 oz (85 g) sugar

3 oz (85 g) finely chopped cucumber

3 tablespoons finely chopped toasted peanuts

1 teaspoon fish sauce

1 small red chili, finely sliced

FISH CAKES

1 lb 20 oz (750 g) firm white fish fillets (such as halibut, snapper, basa), chopped

3 tablespoons Thai red curry paste

3 kaffir lime leaves, torn

3 tablespoons chopped fresh cilantro

1½ tablespoons fish sauce

1 egg

2 tablespoons cornflour

4 oz (115 g) green beans, thinly sliced

3 oz (85 g) thinly sliced spring onions

peanut (or vegetable) oil, for brushing

TO MAKE THE DIPPING SAUCE, combine the vinegar, water, and sugar in a small saucepan. Stir over a medium heat until the sugar has dissolved. Simmer for 2 minutes to thicken slightly then remove from the heat and allow to cool completely. When cool, add the remaining ingredients and stir until combined.

To make the fish cakes, put the fish, curry paste, lime leaves, cilantro, fish sauce, egg, and cornflour in a food processor and blend until smooth. Scrape the mixture into a bowl.

Add the beans and onions to the bowl and stir until well combined. Using wet hands to prevent the mixture from sticking, use two rounded tablespoons of mixture to shape into a fish cake; repeat with the remaining mixture. Brush the fish cakes with oil.

Heat the barbecue to medium-high (about 400°F/200°C/gas mark 6).

Grill the fish cakes for 2–3 minutes on each side until cooked. Serve with the dipping sauce.

MAKES ABOUT 16

HARISSA LEMON SARDINES WITH MINT AND ALMOND COUSCOUS

8 x 2 oz (60 g) fresh sardines, cleaned and gutted
salt and freshly ground black pepper
1 tablespoon olive oil
1 tablespoon harissa paste
1 teaspoon finely grated lemon zest

MINT AND ALMOND COUSCOUS
1 pint (500 ml) chicken stock
2 teaspoons olive oil
1 lb 2 oz (500 g) couscous
salt and freshly ground black pepper
4 oz (115 g) slivered almonds, toasted
a handful of fresh mint, chopped
1 tablespoon lemon juice

HEAT THE BARBECUE TO MEDIUM-HIGH (about 400°F/200°C/gas mark 6) and grease the grill.

Brush the sardines with a little oil then season with salt and pepper. Grill on the barbecue for about 5 minutes on each side until cooked and a little charred.

TO MAKE THE MINT AND ALMOND COUSCOUS, heat the stock and oil in a saucepan until the mixture just comes to the boil. Remove from the heat and stir in the couscous, salt and pepper. Cover and leave to stand for 5 minutes then fluff with a fork. Stir in almonds, mint, and juice. Serve with the sardines.

SERVES 3–4

GRILLED FISH BURGERS

PUT THE FISH, CHEESE, BREADCRUMBS, onions, chili sauce, cilantro, egg, garlic, salt and pepper in a food processor and process until smooth.

Shape the mixture into 6 equal-sized patties. Cover and refrigerate for 30 minutes. Heat a barbecue to medium (about 350°F/180°C/gas mark 4) and grease the grill. Brush the patties with oil and grill for 3–4 minutes on each side until lightly browned.

Place the buns cut-side down on the grill and cook for 1–2 minutes until toasted.

TO MAKE THE CREAM CHEESE SPREAD, mix together the cream cheese and chili sauce until smooth. Add the sour cream and spring onion then stir to combine.

Spread each bun with the cream cheese mixture then fill with fish patties, onion, tomato, and salad leaves.

MAKES 6

1 lb 5 oz (600 g) firm white fish (such as sea bass, cod, or halibut) cut into large pieces
4 oz (115 g) Asiago or Parmesan cheese, grated
4 oz (115 g) fine dry breadcrumbs
2 oz (55 g) spring onions, chopped
2 tablespoons sweet chili sauce
2 tablespoons chopped fresh cilantro
1 egg
2 garlic cloves, crushed
salt and freshly ground black pepper
vegetable oil, for brushing
6 buns, split
6 thin slices red onion, separated
2 tomatoes, sliced
8 oz (225 g) baby salad leaves

CREAM CHEESE SPREAD
4 oz (115 g) cream cheese, softened
2 tablespoons sweet chili sauce
½ cup (115 ml) sour cream
2 tablespoons finely chopped spring onion

CHARGRILLED OCTOPUS

HEAT THE BARBECUE TO MEDIUM-HIGH (about 400°F/200°C/gas mark 6) and grease the grill.

Combine all the ingredients in a bowl.

Cook the octopus on the barbecue for about 10 minutes, turning occasionally, until a little charred and just cooked; do not overcook.

If using a larger octopus, cut into smaller pieces before serving. Serve with lemon wedges.

SERVES 4

⅓ cup (85 ml) tomato ketchup
⅓ cup (85 ml) barbecue sauce
a handful of fresh parsley, chopped
2 tablespoon Worcestershire sauce
2 tablespoons lemon juice
1 teaspoon chili powder
4 garlic cloves, minced
1 lb 10 oz (750 g) medium-large (or baby) octopus, cleaned
lemon wedges, to serve

ORANGE BASIL SALMON WITH MANGO SALSA

To make the orange basil salmon, combine all the ingredients in a large shallow dish or re-sealable plastic bag. Cover or seal and refrigerate for 8 hours or overnight.

To make the mango salsa, put all the ingredients in a large bowl and stir gently to combine.

Drain and discard the salmon marinade. Cook the salmon on the barbecue for about 5 minutes on each side depending on the thickness of the salmon. Serve the salmon with the mango salsa alongside.

SERVES 4

ORANGE BASIL SALMON

1 cup (225 ml) orange juice
1 tablespoon finely grated orange zest
a handful of chopped fresh basil
3 tablespoons honey
1 teaspoon sambal oelek (chili paste)
1 teaspoon ground cumin
1 teaspoon freshly ground black pepper
½ teaspoon salt
4 garlic cloves, crushed
4 salmon fillets (with or without skin)

MANGO SALSA

½ cup (55 ml) lime juice
2 large ripe mangoes, peeled, seeded and chopped
1 red pepper, diced
a handful of fresh cilantro, chopped, plus extra for garnish
1 garlic clove, crushed
½ cup (55 ml) orange juice
1 jalapeño pepper, finely chopped
salt and mixed whole peppercorns

GRILLED SALMON BURGERS

ROASTED RED PEPPER
MAYONNAISE

2 roasted red peppers, seeds
   removed
½ cup (115 ml) good-quality
   mayonnaise
2 tablespoons sweet chili sauce
1 garlic clove, quartered
salt and freshly ground black
   pepper

SALMON BURGERS

4 salmon fillets
2 tablespoons jalapeño (or red
   pepper) jelly, warmed
olive oil
salt and freshly ground black
   pepper
4 wholegrain buns, split
2 tomatoes, sliced
2 handfuls mixed baby lettuce
   leaves
3 oz (85 g) thinly sliced red onion
1 avocado, sliced

To make the roasted pepper mayonnaise put all the ingredients in a food processor and blend until smooth.

To make the salmon burgers, heat the barbecue to medium (about 350°F/180°C/gas mark 4) and grease the grill. Brush the salmon fillets with jalapeño jelly then drizzle with a little olive oil. Season with salt and pepper. Cook on the barbecue for 3–4 minutes on each side.

Place the buns cut-side down on the grill and cook until golden. Spread both cut sides of each bun with red pepper mayonnaise then fill with salmon, tomato, lettuce, onion, and avocado.

Serves 4

VEGETABLES & SIDES

Vegetables are a must for any barbecue, providing different textures, colors, and flavors, plus a healthy accompaniment to all that meat! With classics such as Mac and Cheese and Warm Potato Salad, plus new ideas for beets, butternut squash, couscous, and peppers, these salads, sides, and potato dishes will keep vegetarians happy and even offer dedicated carnivores something to tempt them.

CHEESE QUESADILLAS

PREHEAT THE BARBECUE TO MEDIUM (about 350°F/180°C/gas mark 4) and grease the grill.

Lay 4 tortillas on a chopping board. Spread with the chili jelly then sprinkle with both cheeses. Gently press the remaining tortillas over the cheese.

Brush both sides with oil and grill on the barbecue for about 3 minutes on each side or until crisp and grill marks appear.

Cut into wedges to serve

MAKES 4

8 flour tortillas

3 oz (85 g) red chili jelly

6 oz (170 g) Cheddar cheese, grated

6 oz (170 g) mozzarella cheese, grated

vegetable oil, for brushing

CORN AND TOMATO SALAD WITH CILANTRO DRESSING

1 lb 8 oz (675 g) corn
  (fresh, canned or thawed
  if frozen)
4 tomatoes
2 red onions, finely chopped

CILANTRO DRESSING
¼ cup (55 ml) olive oil
a handful of fresh cilantro,
  coarsely chopped
2 tablespoons coarsely
  chopped mint
2 tablespoons white wine vinegar
1 tablespoon lime juice
2 teaspoons soft brown sugar
1 garlic clove, peeled
salt and freshly ground black
  pepper

STIR TOGETHER THE CORN, TOMATOES, and red onion in a large bowl.

TO MAKE THE CILANTRO DRESSING, put all the ingredients in a food processor and blend until smooth.

Pour the dressing over the corn mixture toss to combine.

SERVES 6

ARUGULA, MINT AND GRILLED POTATO SALAD

To make the honey parmesan dressing, place all the ingredients in a blender and process until smooth.

Preheat the barbecue to medium (about 350°F/180°C/gas mark 4) and grease the grill.

Combine the onion, vinegar and sugar in a bowl; set aside.

Toss the potato slices with oil, garlic, salt and pepper in a bowl. Cook the potato on the barbecue for about 5 minutes on each side until tender and grill marks appear.

Drain the onions from the mixture and gently combine with the warm potato slices, mint, arugula, and dressing in a bowl.

Serves 6

HONEY PARMESAN DRESSING
½ cup (115 ml) good-quality
   mayonnaise
½ cup (115 ml) Parmesan cheese,
   finely grated
3 tablespoons red wine vinegar
2 tablespoons honey
1 garlic clove, crushed
salt and freshly ground black
   pepper

1 small red onion, thinly sliced
2 tablespoons red wine vinegar
1 teaspoon granulated sugar
1 lb 10 oz (750 g) new potatoes,
   thinly sliced
2 tablespoons olive oil
3 garlic cloves, crushed
salt and freshly ground black
   pepper
a large handful of mint leaves,
   torn
1 packet of baby arugula leaves

FRESH TOMATO AND MOZZARELLA SALAD

ARRANGE THE TOMATO SLICES ON A PLATTER. Sprinkle with garlic, basil, salt and pepper. Tear the mozzarella into pieces and place over the tomatoes.

Drizzle everything with oil, vinegar, and lemon juice. Season with a little more salt and pepper if desired. Sprinkle with Parmesan shavings before serving.

SERVES 6

2 lb 4 oz (1 kg) tomatoes, sliced
2 garlic cloves, minced
2 tablespoons chopped fresh basil
salt and freshly ground black
  pepper
1 large ball of fresh mozzarella,
  drained
2 tablespoons olive oil
1 tablespoon balsamic vinegar
1 tablespoon lemon juice
3 oz (85 g) Parmesan cheese
  shavings

PICKLED BEET SALAD

8 beets, trimmed and unpeeled
3 tablespoons white wine vinegar
1½ tablespoons olive oil
1 tablespoon honey
2 teaspoons wholegrain mustard
¼ teaspoon salt
1 tablespoon chopped fresh basil

OLIVE DRESSING

2 oz (55 g) olives of your choice,
  pitted
¼ cup (55 ml) olive oil
2 tablespoons red wine vinegar
1 garlic clove, peeled

Preheat the oven or barbecue to medium-high (about 400°F/200°C/gas mark 6) .

Wrap each beet in aluminum foil and place on a baking sheet. Bake in the oven or on the barbecue for about 1 hour or until softened. Set aside to cool.

Wearing rubber gloves, peel away and discard the skin from each beet. Cut into chunks.

TO MAKE THE OLIVE DRESSING Whisk together the vinegar, oil, honey, mustard, salt, and basil in a medium-sized bowl. Add the beet and toss to combine.

Cover and refrigerate 1 hour or overnight.

SERVES 6

GRILLED ASPARAGUS WITH LEMON CHILI CRUMBS

2 tablespoons butter
12 oz (340 g) fresh breadcrumbs
1 tablespoon lemon zest
1 teaspoon dried chili flakes
olive oil, for drizzling
1 lb 2 oz (500 g) asparagus, trimmed
1 teaspoon garlic salt
½ teaspoon freshly ground pepper

MELT THE BUTTER IN A LARGE FRYING PAN over a medium heat. Add the breadcrumbs. Cook, stirring, for about 3 minutes or until the breadcrumbs are golden and crisp. Add the lemon zest and chili and stir to combine.

Heat the barbecue to medium (about 350°F/180°C/gas mark 4) and grease the grill.

Drizzle a little oil over the asparagus. Season with the garlic, salt and black pepper. Grill on the barbecue for 5–7 minutes, turning occasionally, until tender but still with a little bite.

Serve sprinkled with the warm lemon chili crumbs.

SERVES 4

TOMATO, ROASTED PEPPER, AND BREAD SALAD

BALSAMIC VINAIGRETTE
1 garlic clove, crushed
¼ cup (55 ml) olive oil
2 tablespoons balsamic vinegar
2 tablespoons lemon juice
salt and freshly ground black pepper

2 large peppers, quartered and seeds removed
6 slices crusty bread, such as ciabatta
olive oil
salt and freshly ground black pepper
1 garlic clove, peeled
8 red tomatoes, chopped
8 yellow tomatoes, chopped
a handful of fresh parsley, chopped
2 tablespoons chopped fresh dill

To make the balsamic vinaigrette, place all the ingredients in a screw-top jar and shake until well combined.

Heat the barbecue to medium-high (about 400°F/200°C/gas mark 6) and grease the grill.

Grill the peppers on the barbecue, turning occasionally, until the skin has blistered and blackened. Place in bowl, cover, and set aside. When cool, peel and discard skin. Coarsely chop the peppers and place in a bowl.

Brush both sides of each slice of bread with a little oil and season with salt and pepper. Toast the bread on the barbecue for about 2 minutes on each side or until grill marks appear. Rub garlic over the toasted bread then break into chunks and add to the peppers.

Add the vinaigrette and remaining ingredients to the peppers abd bread mixture. Mix gently to combine.

Serves 4–6

BARBECUED ONION, FENNEL, AND ORANGE SALAD

To make the vinaigrette, place all the ingredients in a screw-top jar and shake until well combined.

Heat the barbecue to medium (about 350°F/180°C/gas mark 4) and grease the grill.

Grill the onion and fennel for about 5 minutes on each side until tender and grill marks appear.

Toss together the onion, fennel, orange segments, and vinaigrette in a large bowl. Sprinkle with almonds to serve.

Serves 4–6

SHALLOT VINAIGRETTE
3 tablespoons olive oil
2 tablespoons finely chopped
   shallots
2 tablespoons red wine vinegar
2 tablespoons red chili jelly
salt and freshly ground black
   pepper
1 garlic clove, crushed

2 red onions, peeled and sliced
   into thick rings
2 fennel bulbs, trimmed and
   sliced
3 large oranges, peeled and
   segmented
4 oz (115 g) sliced almonds,
   toasted, to serve

WARM POTATO SALAD WITH CREAMY MUSTARD DRESSING

CREAMY MUSTARD DRESSING

3 tablespoons sour cream

2 tablespoons white wine vinegar

1 tablespoon wholegrain mustard

1 tablespoon honey

1 garlic clove, crushed

salt and freshly ground black
   pepper

WARM POTATO SALAD

2 lb 4 oz (1 kg) new potatoes

1 tablespoon olive oil

½ teaspoon salt

freshly ground black pepper

1 bunch of spring onions,
   thinly sliced

3 oz (85 g) pine nuts, toasted

To MAKE THE CREAMY MUSTARD DRESSING, whisk together all the ingredients in a bowl then set aside.

To MAKE POTATO SALAD, line a baking sheet with nonstick baking paper. Preheat the oven to 400°F/200°C/gas mark 6. Combine the whole potatoes, oil, and salt and arrange in a single layer on the baking sheet. Roast for about 35 minutes until golden and tender.

Put the potatoes in a bowl and add the remaining salad ingredients. Drizzle with dressing and gently toss to combine. Serve warm or chilled.

SERVES 6

ROASTED BUTTERNUT SQUASH SALAD

To make the maple dressing, place all the ingredients in a screw-top jar and shake until well combined.

To make the roasted butternut squash salad, line a large baking sheet with nonstick baking paper. Heat the oven or barbecue to 400°F/200°C/gas mark 6. Peel the squash, cut in half lengthways, then scrape out and discard the seeds. Cut into ¼ in/6 mm- thick slices.

Combine the squash, chili sauce, oil, rosemary, onion, salt, and pepper on the prepared baking sheet and arrange in a single layer. Roast, uncovered, in the preheated oven (or on the barbecue), turning once during cooking, for 30–40 minutes or until tender and golden. Remove the rosemary.

Place the lettuce, goats' cheese, almonds, and squash mixture in a bowl. Drizzle with the dressing and toss gently.

Serves 6

MAPLE DRESSING
2 tablespoons olive oil
2 tablespoons white wine vinegar
2 tablespoons maple syrup
2 teaspoons Dijon mustard
salt and freshly ground black
  pepper

ROASTED BUTTERNUT SQUASH
SALAD
2 lb 12 oz (1.25 kg) butternut
  squash
3 tablespoons sweet chili sauce
2 teaspoons olive oil
2 sprigs rosemary
1 red onion, cut into thin wedges
salt and freshly ground black
  pepper
a large packet of mixed baby
  lettuce leaves
4 oz (125 g) goats' cheese,
  crumbled
3 oz (85 g) sliced almonds,
  toasted

BEET, SPINACH, AND CANDIED WALNUT SALAD

6 beets, trimmed
1 large packet of baby spinach
  leaves
8 oz (225 g) Parmesan cheese
  shavings

CANDIED WALNUTS
1 egg white
a pinch of ground cinnamon
3 oz (85 g) sugar
8 oz (225 g) walnuts

VINAIGRETTE
2 tablespoons finely chopped
  shallots
⅓ cup (85 ml) olive oil
2 tablespoons white wine vinegar
1 tablespoon honey
salt and cracked black pepper

PREHEAT THE OVEN TO 375°F/190°C/gas mark 5.

Wrap each beet in aluminum foil and place on a baking sheet. Bake in the oven or on the barbecue for about 1 hour or until softened. Set aside and leave to cool. Wearing rubber gloves, peel away and discard the skin from each beet. Cut into chunks.

TO MAKE THE CANDIED WALNUTS, line a baking sheet with nonstick baking paper. Whisk together the egg white, cinnamon, and sugar in medium-sized bowl. Add the walnuts and stir to coat. Spread the mixture onto the baking sheet. Cook in the oven for about 20 minutes, stirring occasionally, or until golden. Once cool, chop the walnut mixure.

TO MAKE THE VINAIGRETTE, place all the ingredients in a screw-top jar and shake until well combined.

Toss together the beet, spinach, Parmesan, and candied walnuts. Drizzle with vinaigrette.

SERVES 6

ROASTED SWEET POTATO AND SPINACH SALAD

To MAKE THE BASIL MAPLE DRESSING, place all the ingredients in a blender and process until smooth.

Line a large baking sheet with nonstick baking paper. Preheat the oven to 375°F/190°C/gas mark 5. Combine the sweet potato, oil, salt and pepper on the baking sheet. Roast for about 50 minutes or until tender and golden. Allow to cool slightly.

Toss the sweet potatoes in a bowl with the dressing and remaining ingredients. Serve immediately.

SERVES 4–6

BASIL MAPLE DRESSING
⅓ cup (85 ml) olive oil
3 tablespoons cider vinegar
1 tablespoon maple syrup
2 tablespoons chopped fresh basil
1 garlic clove, peeled
salt and freshly ground black
  pepper

1 lb 2 oz (500 g) sweet potato,
  peeled and chopped
1 tablespoon olive oil
salt and freshly ground black
  pepper
4 handfuls of baby spinach leaves
4 oz (115 g) sliced almonds,
  toasted
4 oz (115 g) dried cherries (or
  cranberries)

FATTOUSH (PITA SALAD)

TO MAKE THE LEMON DRESSING, place all the ingredients in a screw-top jar and shake until well combined.

Preheat the oven, or barbecue, to 400°F/200°C/gas mark 6. Brush the pita breads with oil and place on a baking sheet. Cook or grill for 5–10 minutes or until golden. Allow to cool then break into pieces and set aside.

Combine the remaining salad ingredients in a bowl. Add the dressing and toss to combine. Add the bread pieces just before serving.

SERVES 4–6

LEMON DRESSING
⅓ cup (85 ml) lemon juice
¼ cup (55 ml) olive oil
2 garlic cloves, crushed
salt and freshly ground black
    pepper
¼ teaspoon ground cumin

2 large pita breads
2 teaspoons olive oil
1 cucumber, chopped
4 tomatoes, chopped
1 green pepper, chopped
8 spring onions, thinly sliced
a handful of fresh mint leaves,
    chopped
a handful of fresh parsley,
    chopped
2 tablespoons chopped fresh
    cilantro

BEET, CARROT, AND QUINOA SALAD

MAPLE APPLE VINAIGRETTE
⅓ cup (85 ml) olive oil
3 tablespoons apple cider vinegar
   (or white wine vinegar)
2 tablespoons lemon juice
2 tablespoons Dijon mustard
2 tablespoons maple syrup
salt and freshly ground black
   pepper

8 oz (225 g) quinoa
1 pint (500 ml) water
12 oz (340 g) grated carrot
12 oz (340 g) diced apple
8 oz (225 g) dark raisins
8 oz (225 g) sliced almonds,
   toasted
8 oz (225 g) pumpkin seeds,
   toasted
1 bunch spring onions, thinly
   sliced
salt and freshly ground black
   pepper
12 oz (340 g) grated beet

To make the vinaigrette, place all the ingredients in a screw-top jar and shake until well combined.

Place the quinoa in a sieve and rinse under the cold tap until the water runs clear. Place in medium-sized saucepan and add water. Bring to the boil over a high heat, then reduce the heat to medium-low. Simmer, partially covered, for 10–15 minutes or until all the water has been absorbed. Fluff with a fork. Rinse well again then drain well and set aside to cool.

Combine the cooled quinoa, carrot, apple, raisins, almonds, pumpkin seeds, spring onions, and a pinch of salt and pepper in a large bowl. Drizzle with the vinaigrette and toss gently to combine. Add the beet and stir gently.

Serves 6

BROWN BUTTER MASHED POTATOES

3 lb 5 oz (1.5 kg) potatoes, peeled and quartered (about 6 large potatoes)

generous pinch of salt

4 oz (115 g) butter

½ teaspoon finely ground white pepper

⅓ cup (85 ml) heavy cream, warmed

PLACE THE POTATOES IN A LARGE SAUCEPAN. Cover with water and add the salt. Cook over a medium-high heat for about 25 minutes or until the potatoes are tender. Drain well and return to pan. Mash with a potato masher to remove any large lumps.

Heat the butter in a small saucepan over a medium heat until the butter is golden brown. Add to the potatoes with the remaining ingredients. Stir vigorously with a fork until all lumps are removed.

SERVES 8

MAC AND CHEESE

COOK THE PASTA IN A LARGE SAUCEPAN of salted, boiling water for about 12 minutes or until tender. Drain well then return the pasta to the saucepan.

Meanwhile, heat the butter in a large saucepan over a medium heat. Add the flour and stir for 1 minute. Gradually stir in the milk and stir until the sauce boils and thickens. Reduce the heat to medium-low and simmer, uncovered, for 5 minutes or until thickened, stirring occasionally.

Remove the sauce from the heat and stir in the remaining ingredients. Add the sauce to the pasta and stir until combined.

SERVES 4–6

12 oz (375 g) fusilli (or macaroni) pasta
2 tablespoons butter
2 tablespoons plain flour
2 teaspoons Dijon mustard
1 pint (500 ml) milk
8 oz (225 g) Cheddar, grated
4 oz (115 g) fresh Parmesan cheese, grated
pinch of ground nutmeg
salt and freshly ground black pepper

WARM PEA SALAD WITH HAZELNUT BUTTER

MELT THE BUTTER IN A SAUCEPAN over a medium heat. Add the hazelnuts and cook, stirring occasionally, until the butter is golden brown.

Meanwhile, bring a saucepan of salted water to the boil. Cook the sugar snap peas and Snow Pea in the pan for about 3 minutes. Add the peas and cook for 3–5 minutes until tender. Drain well.

Return the peas to the saucepan. Add the butter mixture and stir to coat.

SERVES 8

3 tablespoons butter

3 oz (85 g) hazelnuts, toasted, peeled and coarsely chopped

salt and freshly ground black pepper

1 lb 2 oz (500 g) sugar snap peas, trimmed

1 lb 2 oz (500 g) Snow Pea, trimmed

1 lb 4 oz (565 g) fresh or frozen garden peas

COUSCOUS, WALNUT, AND ZUCCHINI SALAD

ORANGE, HONEY AND MINT DRESSING

¼ cup (55 ml) olive oil

a handful of fresh mint, chopped

3 tablespoons orange juice

2 tablespoons lemon juice

1 teaspoon finely grated orange zest

2 tablespoons honey

salt and freshly ground black pepper

COUSCOUS SALAD

3 zucchini, cut lengthways into ½ in/1 cm-thick slices

olive oil, for brushing, plus 1 tablespoon extra

1¼ pints (700 ml) chicken stock

1 lb 9 oz (700 g) couscous

salt and freshly ground black pepper

8 oz (225 g) walnuts, toasted and coarsely chopped

8 oz (225 g) dark raisins

TO MAKE THE ORANGE, HONEY, AND MINT DRESSING, place all the ingredients in a screw-top jar and shake until well combined.

TO MAKE THE COUSCOUS SALAD, heat a barbecue or grill to medium-high. Brush the zucchini with a little olive oil. Grill for about 3 minutes on each side until grill marks appear then remove from the grill and coarsely chop.

Place the stock in a large saucepan and heat over a medium-high heat until boiling. Remove from the heat and immediately stir in the couscous and extra oil. Cover and allow to stand for 8 minutes.

Fluff up the couscous with a fork. Add the dressing, zucchini, and remaining ingredients and stir until well combined.

SERVES 4–6

GREEK-STYLE SALAD

6 tomatoes, cubed
1 cucumber, halved lengthways
    and thickly sliced
2 green peppers, chopped
8 oz (250 g) feta cheese, coarsely
    crumbled
20 Kalamata olives
1 packet of mixed lettuce leaves
    (such as romaine, escarole, or
    frisée)

DRESSING
½ cup (115 ml) olive oil
3 tablespoons lemon juice
1 tablespoon dried oregano
2 garlic cloves, crushed
salt and freshly ground black
    pepper

PUT ALL THE SALAD INGREDIENTS in a large bowl.

TO MAKE THE DRESSING, put all the ingredients in a screw-top jar and shake until well combined.

Drizzle the dressing over the salad and gently toss to combine.

SERVES 6

MIXED POTATO BAKE

GREASE A SHALLOW OVENPROOF DISH. Preheat oven to 350°F/180°C/gas mark 4.

Layer half of the potato and sweet potato in the greased dish then scatter over half the bacon and cheese. Repeat the layers and season with salt, pepper and nutmeg.

Pour the cream over the potatoes. Bake, uncovered, for about an hour or until the potatoes are tender and the top is golden brown.

Cover and leave to stand for 10 minutes before serving.

SERVES 8–10

2 lb 12 oz (1.25 kg) red potatoes, peeled and thinly sliced

1 lb 10 oz (750 g) sweet potatoes, peeled and thinly sliced

10 bacon slices, coarsely chopped and cooked until golden

12 oz (340 g) Cheddar cheese, grated

½ teaspoon salt

¼ teaspoon freshly ground black pepper

½ teaspoon ground nutmeg

1 pint (500 ml) heavy cream

ROASTED LEMON AND ROSEMARY SWEET POTATOES

HEAT THE BARBECUE TO MEDIUM-HIGH (about 400°F/200°C/gas mark 6).

Grease a large sheet of heavy-duty aluminum foil. Combine all of the ingredients in a bowl then arrange on the foil. Fold the foil around the sweet potato to form a parcel.

Reduce the barbecue temperature to medium (about 350°F/180°C/gas mark 4). Place the foil on the upper rack and cook the potatoes for 50–60 minutes, turning occasionally, until tender on the inside and crisp on the outside.

SERVES 6

2 lb 4 oz (1 kg) sweet potatoes, cubed
2 tablespoons olive oil
1 tablespoon finely grated lemon zest
3 rosemary stalks
4 garlic cloves, bruised
salt and cracked black pepper

ROASTED PEPPERS WITH BASIL, BALSAMIC, AND GOATS' CHEESE

4 large red peppers
4 large yellow peppers
2 tablespoons olive oil
salt and freshly ground black
    pepper
a handful of basil leaves,
    shredded
1 tablespoon balsamic vinegar
4 oz (125 g) goats' cheese
crusty bread, to serve

HEAT A BARBECUE TO MEDIUM-HIGH (about 400°F/200°C/gas mark 6).

Grill the peppers for about 10 minutes, turning occasionally, until the skin has blistered and blackened. Place the peppers in a bowl, cover and leave to stand for 10 minutes.

Peel away and discard the skin from the peppers. Cut open each pepper then scrape out and discard the seeds and membranes. Cut the peppers into wide strips and combine with the oil, salt and pepper in a bowl.

Arrange the peppers on a platter and sprinkle with basil and vinegar. Break the cheese into small pieces and scatter over the peppers.

Serve with crusty bread.

SERVES 6

GRILLED LEMON AND POTATO SKEWERS

3 tablespoons sweet chili sauce

2 teaspoons finely grated lemon
  zest

2 tablespoons lemon juice

salt and freshly ground black
  pepper

24–30 new potatoes

6–8 large metal skewers

COMBINE THE CHILI SAUCE, LEMON ZEST, lemon juice, salt and pepper in a small bowl; set aside.

Cook the potatoes in a large saucepan of salted water for about 12 minutes or until almost tender. Drain well.

Heat the barbecue to high (about 425°F/220°C/gas mark 7) and grease the grill.

Thread the potatoes onto metal skewers.

Reduce the barbecue heat to medium-low (about 325°F/160°C/gas mark 2½). Cook the potato skewers with the lid closed for about 10 minutes, turning occasionally and brushing with lemon mixture. Remove from the grill when the potatoes are cooked through and grill marks appear.

MAKES 6–8

PEANUT BUTTER HUMMUS

PUT ALL THE INGREDIENTS IN A FOOD processor and blend until smooth.

Add a little water to reach the desired consistency if the mixture is too thick.

Makes about 1½ cups (340 ml).

1 x 14 oz (400 g) can chickpeas, rinsed and drained

3 tablespoons smooth peanut butter

¼ cup (55 ml) lemon juice

2 garlic cloves, crushed

2 tablespoons olive oil

¼ teaspoon smoky paprika

salt and freshly ground black pepper

SWEET CREAMY COLESLAW

COMBINE THE MAYONNAISE, SUGAR, vinegar, and salt in a bowl. Add the remaining ingredients and stir to combine. Cover and refrigerate.

This coleslaw is best made at least 3 hours ahead. Stir just before serving.

SERVES 4–6

¾ cup (170 ml) good-quality mayonnaise

3 oz (55 g) sugar

¼ cup (55 ml) white wine vinegar

salt, to taste

2 lb (900 g) finely shredded cabbage

1 large carrot, grated

6 spring onions, thinly sliced

CORN PUDDING

1 x 14 oz (400 g) can corn, drained

1 x 14 oz (400 g) can creamed corn

½ cup (115 ml) sour cream

3 oz (85 g) dried breadcrumbs

1 egg

salt and freshly ground black pepper

PREHEAT THE OVEN TO 350°F/180°C/gas mark 4.

Grease a shallow ovenproof dish.

Combine all the ingredients in a bowl then scrape the mixture into the dish. Bake, uncovered, for about 45 minutes or until golden and set.

SERVES 4

MARINADES & RUBS

Marinades and rubs are what separate good barbecues from great ones. Adding flavor, tenderness, and moisture, marinades can be made from almost anything, including herbs, spices, honey, garlic, and wine. These recipes are an ideal starting point for your own marinating experiments and can be adapted to suit your tastes. Also included in this chapter are recipes for lip-smacking sauces, chutneys, and relishes to accompany grilled meats, fish, and vegetables.

MAYONNAISE

THIS MAYONNAISE CAN BE FLAVORED with herbs, horseradish, sweet chili sauce, spices, honey, wasabi…the list is endless.

Put the yolks, lemon juice, vinegar, sugar, and salt in a blender and process until smooth.

With the motor still running, add the oil in a slow, steady stream through the liquids funnel until the mixture is thick and pale. This step should take about 5 minutes.

Spoon the mixture into clean jars and store in the refrigerator.

Will keep for 2 weeks.

MAKES ABOUT 1½ CUPS (340 ML)

3 egg yolks
1½ tablespoons lemon juice
1½ tablespoons white wine vinegar
½ teaspoon sugar
salt, to taste
1½ cups (340 ml) vegetable oil (or light olive oil)

BASIL CHILI MARINADE

⅓ cup (85 ml) dry white wine
3 tablespoons chopped fresh basil
1 tablespoon wholegrain mustard
2 tablespoons olive oil
1 teaspoon sambal oelek
   (chili paste)
2 garlic cloves, crushed

These quantites are enough
to marinate about 1 lb 2 oz
(500 g) of meat.

COMBINE ALL THE INGREDIENTS IN A large glass bowl or re-sealable plastic (freezer) bag.

Add your favorite meat to the bowl or bag and stir or shake to coat completely in the marinade. Cover or seal. Marinate in the refrigerator for about 8 hours or ideally overnight.

Remove the meat and discard any leftover marinade.

Grill the marinated meat on the barbecue.

WARM SPICE RUB

STIR ALL THE INGREDIENTS TOGETHER in a bowl. Rub the mixture all over the meat of your choice. Cover and marinate in the refrigerator for 3 hours, or ideally overnight, before barbecuing.

MAKE AHEAD: This rub can be made up to 2 weeks in advance and stored in an airtight container in the refrigerator.

MAKES ABOUT 6 oz (170 G)

1 small onion, chopped
2 tablespoons lemon juice
4 garlic cloves, crushed
1 tablespoon white vinegar
1 tablespoon olive oil
1 tablespoon salt
½ teaspoon ground black pepper
½ teaspoon cayenne pepper
½ teaspoon cinnamon
¼ teaspoon nutmeg
¼ teaspoon ground cloves

These quantities will make enough rub to cover about 1 lb 10 oz (750 g) of meat.

CRANBERRY WINE SAUCE

3 oz (85 g) cranberry jelly
⅓ cup (85 ml) dry white wine
¾ cup (170 ml) chicken stock
1 rosemary sprig
¼ teaspoon salt
¼ teaspoon freshly ground black pepper
1 teaspoon cornflour
1 tablespoon water
1 tablespoon butter

PUT ALL THE INGREDIENTS EXCEPT for the butter in a frying pan. Stir over a medium heat until the cranberry jelly has melted. Allow to simmer, uncovered, for 10 minutes.

Combine the cornflour and water in a small bowl. Stir into the sauce and continue stirring until thickened slightly.

Whisk in the butter and stir until melted.

SERVES 4–6

LEMONGRASS AND LIME MARINADE

¼ cup (55 ml) lime juice

a handful of fresh cilantro, chopped

3 tablespoons sweet chili sauce

2 tablespoons canola (or peanut) oil

2 tablespoons finely chopped lemongrass

1 tablespoon finely chopped fresh ginger

2 teaspoons finely grated lime zest

1 teaspoon sesame oil

2 garlic cloves, crushed

2 teaspoons fish sauce

These quantities will make enough marinade to cover about 1 lb 2 oz (500 g) of meat.

MIX ALL THE INGREDIENTS TOGETHER in a glass bowl or re-sealable plastic (freezer) bag. Add the meat of your choice to the marinade and stir or toss to combine. Cover or seal.

Marinate in the refrigerator for 8 hours or ideally overnight.

Remove the meat and discard any remaining marinade before barbecuing.

MAKES ABOUT ½ CUP (115 ML)

CHILI RUB

STIR ALL THE INGREDIENTS TOGETHER in a bowl.

Rub the mixture over the meat of your choice, making sure that it is coated all over. Cover and marinate in the refrigerator for 3 hours, or ideally overnight, before barbecuing.

MAKES ABOUT 3 oz (85 G)

1½ tablespoon chili powder
1 tablespoon garlic powder
1 tablespoon dried oregano
1 tablespoon paprika
1 teaspoon salt
1 teaspoon freshly ground black
    pepper
1½ teaspoons sugar

These quantities will make
enough rub to cover about
1 lb 10 oz (750 g) of meat.

CITRUS SPICE RUB

1 tablespoon soft brown sugar
1 tablespoon finely grated orange
 zest
1 teaspoon lemon zest
1 teaspoon salt
1 teaspoon ground cilantro
1 teaspoon garlic powder
1 teaspoon ground cumin
½ teaspoon freshly ground
  black pepper

These quantities will make
enough rub to cover about
1 lb 10 oz (750 g) of meat.

STIR ALL THE INGREDIENTS TOGETHER in a bowl.

Rub the mixture all over the meat of your choice, making sure that every part is covered. Cover the bowl and marinate in the refrigerator for 3 hours, or overnight if possible, before barbecuing.

MAKES ABOUT ⅓ CUP (85 ML)

MARMALADE AND MUSTARD GLAZE

COMBINE ALL THE INGREDIENTS in a saucepan. Stir over a medium-low heat for about 3 minutes or until the marmalade has melted.

Brush the glaze over your favorite meat during the last 10 minutes of cooking time.

MAKES ABOUT ½ CUP (115 ML)

3 oz (85 g) orange marmalade

2 tablespoons wholegrain mustard

1 tablespoon Worcestershire sauce

1 tablespoon onion powder

1 garlic clove, crushed

¼ teaspoon freshly ground black pepper

These quantities will make enough glaze to cover about 1 lb 7 oz (650 g) of meat.

PEACH CHUTNEY

8 medium firm, ripe peaches
1 medium onion, chopped
8 oz (225 g) sugar
1 cup (225 ml) white wine
  vinegar
1 teaspoon salt
1 teaspoon dried chili flakes

IF FRESH PEACHES AREN'T IN SEASON use thawed, frozen peaches instead.

Cut a cross on the bottom of each peach. Bring a large saucepan of water to the boil then immerse the peaches in the boiling water. Blanch for 1–3 minutes until the skin starts to peel away easily when tested. Remove to a bowl of cold water.

Remove the skin from the peaches. Cut the peaches in half and remove the stones. Coarsely chop the fruit.

Combine the peaches with the remaining ingredients in the same saucepan. Stir over a medium–high heat until the sugar has dissolved. Boil, uncovered, for 15–20 minutes, stirring occasionally, until thickened.

Spoon the hot chutney into warm sterilized jars.

MAKES ABOUT 1¾ PINTS (1 LITRE)

RICH TOMATO SAUCE

GREASE A WIRE RACK AND PLACE on a baking sheet lined with nonstick paper. Preheat the oven to 350°F/180°C/gas mark 4.

Place the tomatoes cut-side up on the prepared rack and season with salt and pepper. Roast for about 2 hours or until the tomatoes are wilted and lightly browned. Remove from the oven and put into a food processor.

Heat the oil in a frying pan. Add the onion and garlic and fry for about 5 minutes or until softened, stirring occasionally. Add the mixture to the food processor.

Add the remaining ingredients and process until smooth.

SERVES 8–12

10 tomatoes, halved lengthways
1 tablespoon olive oil
8 oz (225 g) chopped onion
2 garlic cloves, crushed
2 tablespoons tomato paste
1 teaspoon balsamic vinegar
1 teaspoon soft brown sugar
½ teaspoon salt
¼ teaspoon freshly ground black pepper

MUSHROOM MUSTARD SAUCE

1 tablespoon butter
2 teaspoons canola (or vegetable)
   oil
1 lb 2 oz (500 g) sliced
   mushrooms
2 garlic cloves, crushed
2 tablespoons plain flour
1 cup (225 ml) chicken stock
2 tablespoons sour cream
2 teaspoons Dijon mustard
salt and freshly ground black
   pepper

HEAT THE BUTTER AND OIL IN A frying pan over a medium-high heat. Add the mushrooms and garlic and cook, stirring occasionally, for about 5 minutes or until the mushrooms are softened.

Stir in the flour and stir for 1 minute to cook the flour.

Add the remaining ingredients and boil gently, uncovered, stirring occasionally, for about 5 minutes or until thickened.

SERVES 6–8

CREAMY DILL AND HORSERADISH SAUCE

MELT THE BUTTER IN A SAUCEPAN over a medium heat. Add the shallot and fry for about 3 minutes or until softened.

Stir in the flour and stir for 1 minute over the heat to cook.

Add the sherry and stir until the sauce has thickened. Add the remaining ingredients and stir until combined. Allow to simmer, uncovered, for about 5 minutes or until thickened slightly.

SERVES 4–6

2 tablespoons butter
2 tablespoons finely chopped shallot
1 tablespoon plain flour
2 tablespoons dry sherry
1 cup (225 ml) heavy cream
2 tablespoons creamed horseradish
2 tablespoons chopped fresh dill
salt and freshly ground black pepper

PESTO, WINE, AND GARLIC MARINADE

3 oz (85 g) basil pesto
⅓ cup (85 ml) dry white wine
1 tablespoon olive oil
1 tablespoon balsamic vinegar
6 garlic cloves, crushed
½ teaspoon salt
½ teaspoon freshly ground black
   pepper

These quantities will make enough marinade to cover about 1 lb 2 oz (500 g) of meat.

MIX ALL THE INGREDIENTS TOGETHER in a glass bowl or re-sealable plastic (freezer) bag.

Add your favorite meat to the marinade. Stir or toss to coat the meat in the marinade. Cover or seal.

Marinate for about 8 hours or ideally overnight.

Remove the meat and discard any remaining marinade before barbecuing.

MAKES ABOUT ¾ CUP (175 ML)

BALSAMIC AND ROSEMARY MARINADE

MIX ALL THE INGREDIENTS TOGETHER in a glass bowl or re-sealable plastic (freezer) bag. Add the meat of your choice and stir or toss to combine. Cover or seal.

Marinate in the refrigerator for 8 hours or ideally overnight.

Remove the meat and discard any remaining marinade before barbecuing.

MAKES ABOUT ½ CUP (115 ML)

¼ cup (55 ml) olive oil
¼ cup (55 ml) balsamic vinegar
2 rosemary sprigs
1 tablespoon soft brown sugar
½ teaspoon freshly ground
   black pepper
6 garlic cloves, coarsely chopped

These quantities will make enough marinade to cover about 1 lb 2 oz (500 g) of meat.

SPICY ONION AND TOMATO RELISH

6 tomatoes

2 onions

2 teaspoons salt

2 teaspoons curry powder

9¾ oz (275 g) soft brown sugar

½ cup (115 ml) red wine vinegar

⅓ cup (85 ml) lemon juice

1 tablespoon tomato purée

2 teaspoons dried mustard

½ teaspoon ground cinnamon

CAREFULLY PLACE THE TOMATOES into a large saucepan of boiling water for about 3 minutes or until the skins are starting to peel off.

Remove to a bowl of cold water and allow to stand for 10 minutes. Peel away and discard the skin then chop the tomatoes.

Mix together the tomatoes and remaining ingredients in a large saucepan. Bring to the boil then reduce the heat to medium. Simmer, uncovered, for about 30 minutes or until thickened, stirring occasionally.

Spoon into warm sterilized jars.

MAKES ABOUT 2½ PINTS (1.4 LITRES)

GINGER AND SOY MARINADE

MIX ALL THE INGREDIENTS TOGETHER in a glass bowl or re-sealable plastic (freezer) bag. Add the meat of your choice and stir or toss to combine. Cover or seal.

Marinate in the refrigerator for 8 hours or ideally overnight.

Remove the meat and discard any remaining marinade before barbecuing.

MAKES ABOUT ¾ CUP (170 ML)

1 tablespoon finely grated ginger
2 garlic cloves, crushed
1 tablespoon canola oil
½ teaspoon Chinese Five spice powder
¼ cup (55 ml) soy sauce
1 tablespoon rice vinegar (or white wine vinegar)
2 oz (55 g) finely chopped shallot
1 tablespoon honey

These quantities will make enough marinade to cover about 1 lb 2 oz (500 g) of meat.

INDEX